table of contents

Double-Duty Weeknight Dinners . . . 47

Party at My Place . . . 81

FOREWORD BY JAMIE OLIVER

What an absolute pleasure to be writing this foreword for the one and only Miss Amber Kelley. Amber is a super-enthusiastic little powerhouse, and she's a real joy to cook with. I first came across Amber back in 2013 when she entered our "Search for a Food Tube Star" award at the very young age of 10, and boy did she make an impact!

We had a really memorable day shooting a few recipes together, and I was really struck by how much Amber clearly loves cooking, and particularly loves cooking good food for the people she loves. What impressed me then, and is still very evident now, is Amber's passion and excitement about getting other kids to get in the kitchen and give cooking a go, something I'm very passionate about.

Cooking from scratch is something everyone can (and should!) enjoy, at any age. Amber's beautiful book is bursting with great ideas that make healthy eating a joy—and she's done a great job covering all the bases that, in my experience, teens and kids really want. The recipes are fun to make, and great for sharing. I know my lot at home will go mad for the Fronanas (page 37) for instance! And there's loads of other useful tips and advice that I know will really resonate, such as Amber's lovely ideas for an easy morning routine.

Those all-important teenage years can be a challenge to navigate, but armed with a solid collection of healthy, fun, joyful food hopefully you've got a bit of a head start. Food and cooking has a big role to play in helping us all live happier, healthier lives—and anything that gets us into the kitchen at an early age, and enjoying properly good food, is a brilliant thing.

From day one, Amber's friendly approach and her infectious smile has made her one to watch. Her colorful, fresh food always hits the mark and I'm so excited that she's now able to share all of that in this brilliant book. Guys, you don't need any more encouragement—turn the page and get stuck into these brilliant recipes. Well done, Amber, it's a beaut.

Big love, Jamie O XXX

introduction

I LOVE COOKING. I love the look on people's faces when they try something I made and like it. I love the creativity of experimenting with different recipes and ingredients, and I love dancing around the kitchen, music blaring, house smelling amazing, and just making something delicious with my own hands.

I have been cooking for as long as I can remember, really. My mom taught me to cook because the only thing she knew how to do by the time she got to college was mince garlic, so she wanted my sister and me to learn to cook . . . because you gotta cook to eat, and you gotta eat to live. She thought of cooking as a life skill, like how to do laundry (which she also taught us how to do, and I don't enjoy that nearly as much!).

But it turns out that cooking is more than that. For me, it's a gateway to so many things—energy, fun with friends and family, a strong body, and clean skin—everything a teenager wants.

More and more, you see kids and teens cooking . . . and why not? We are capable, and we want to have a say in what we eat, just like adults.

So, this book is about taking control of your teen years. It's about making easy, mouthwatering dishes that you can be proud of. It's about throwing parties with your friends with food that you all can make together. It's about prepping your own delicious school lunches and snacks so you're never starving. It's about using the power of food to help you be strong and have glowing hair and skin. Really, it's about feeling strong, feeling good, and feeling like "I've got this!"

If you picked up this book out of curiosity and have never heard of me, you may be wondering why I have any expertise in writing a cookbook. I didn't go to culinary school (I'm too young). My parents aren't celebrity chefs, either. But my passion to share my love of cooking and eating wholesome, delicious food has lead me to a seat next to the first lady at the White House, to national television appearances, to cooking collaborations with celebrity chefs, to my own web series on Food Network—and, most important, it's allowed me to connect with so many of you guys. And it's very clear: we all need a book like this!

My wild adventures with cooking didn't start so rosy, however.

When I fell in love with cooking as a little kid, I only thought of it as a fun activity where I got to eat my results (how can you not love that?!). That was until second grade, when I got bullied because the food I brought to school wasn't "cool." The so-called cool foods were all prepackaged—you know, those foods that have flashy colors and all those crazy cartoon characters. Now, my homemade school lunches were absolutely delicious, but my classmates assumed that if it wasn't prepackaged, then it wasn't cool. I was confused and hurt, and I would often come home crying because my classmates didn't like my lunch.

Then, one day, I had a brilliant idea. I remember telling my mom, "You need to become a Food Network star and cook all of our family recipes to prove my friends wrong!" But her answer was (and I quote), "I'm too busy to be a Food Network Star." Pretty hilarious, looking back on it now. But that was a good thing, because I decided then and there that I would just do it myself.

One night, I asked my mom to film me making dinner and we published it on You-Tube. It turns out my grandma wasn't the only one interested in our homemade videos and our YouTube channel grew. Then, I started doing weekly cooking segments at our local news stations, making national TV appearances, and just this past year, I achieved my dream to become the first ever "Food Network Star Kid." But most important, I was thrilled to find there were many others who agreed that "being healthy is cool" and who loved the family recipes I was sharing.

Now, I'm a teenager, and while I no longer have friends bullying me about my homemade food, I have other challenges I face. It's hard to juggle school, homework,

afterschool sports, hanging with friends—and to have the energy to do it all. And let's be honest: hormones are no fun, with mood swings and acne and feeling out of control most of the time.

Cooking and food was the tool that I used to meet my challenge in second grade, and it's the same tool I use to face my challenges as a teenager! It connects me with my friends and family, it helps me combat my mood swings and acne, and it gives me energy to play volleyball, hang with friends, and makes me feel and look my best.

This is more than a cookbook. It's a book about being a teen and how we can use cooking and food to enjoy every day of it. Being a teen isn't easy, but with a fully stocked fridge and this book, we are going to master our teen years one recipe at a time.

Tips for Beginner Cooks

This book is for everyone, including those who are just getting into the awesome world of cooking. I know the whole food world can be really intimidating, but it doesn't have to be hard! Here are some of my top tips to help you get started:

COOK FOODS THAT YOU WANT TO EAT! Not gonna lie: one of the best parts about cooking is getting to eat the end result. So, when you cook foods that you enjoy, it makes the whole process a lot more fun and rewarding.

GO SIMPLE. Not all delicious dishes need a huge list of fancy ingredients. Sometimes the tastiest dishes are the ones made with a few simple fresh ingredients. Starting simple is a perfect way to ease into cooking. Once you get more comfortable, you can choose to explore more complex dishes (but only if you want to!).

CHEAT. Yes, you heard me. But not in school. Cheat when cooking! It's totally okay to find shortcuts to make the job easier. Whether that be using an onion chopper to cut your onions, using your hands to tear lettuce instead of having to use a chef's knife, or even using kitchen scissors to cut herbs, if you can find a way to make your life easier when cooking, do it!

ASK FOR HELP. No, it is not lame to ask for help. When I started cooking, I couldn't even reach the kitchen counter. Asking for help will not only make it easier, but it will also help you in the long run! Learning from others is a huge key to growing your skills and improving.

HAVE FUN! Cooking is one of my favorite things to do, and I want you all to enjoy it, too! Play some music, dance around the kitchen, do whatever you want. As long as you're having fun and eating good food, my mission is accomplished.

What About Knife Skills?

The biggest fear for most of us (and our parents) is that we'll kill ourselves with kitchen knives. True, they can be dangerous . . . but only if you don't know how to use them. My mentor Jamie Oliver talked to me about the importance of learning to handle a knife correctly, because that's the key to safety. I totally agree, and I also think that you don't need a bunch of fancy knife skills to create a masterpiece dish—there are amazing ways to cheat (see point #3 above)!

If you want to use a knife, then think about these tips:

· Always have the knife pointed down at your side when walking.
· Put the flat side of your vegetable or fruit on the cutting board, so you have a stable surface.
· Put a wet paper towel under your cutting board so it doesn't move.
· Take a knife skills class. The way you hold the knife, place your fingers, and the type of food you're cutting are all really important and hard to learn from just pictures in a book or a YouTube video. Look for a class in your area and gain skills that will last you a lifetime.

If you want to

Chop or dice vegetables or curly parsley	Use an onion chopper
Mince garlic	Use a garlic press
Slice vegetables	Use a mandoline
Chop herbs or chiffonade basil	Use kitchen shears
Cut chicken into bite-size pieces	Use kitchen shears
Chop lettuce or greens	Use your hands to tear the leaves

And while we're at it, here is a glossary of the most common cutting terms:

CHOP: cut into bite-size pieces, about 1 inch/2.5 cm

CUBE: cut into little cubes, about ½ to 1 inch/1.5 to 2.5 cm

DICE: chop into tiny cubes, about ⅛ to ¼ inch/3 to 6 mm

MINCE: chop as finely as possible, at most ⅛ inch/3 mm

JULIENNE: cut into matchsticks

CHIFFONADE: cut into thin ribbons

SLICE: cut into flat, thin pieces

It's Getting Hot in Here!

Heat is pure magic—it transforms ingredients into warm, bubbly scrumptiousness. But it can be intimidating to use the stove or oven at first. Here are some ways you can get that magic without any drama:

· Get the lowdown on how your stove and ovens work from an experienced cook, and start by cooking *with* them so you are confident you know the equipment's range's ins and outs.

· Tie long hair back. I have long hair and so does my sister. Tying your hair back keeps it out of your face, and out of the flames.

· Use oven gloves when taking stuff in and out of the oven. I love using oven gloves rather than pot holders or oven mitts, because your entire hand and wrist are covered, and you don't have to worry about the pot holder slipping.

· Stay in the kitchen. Never leave a hot stove unattended!

nourishing breakfasts

Get Ready for School

Not only will these meals pump you up and give you energy to kick-start your day, but they will make you *want* to get out of bed.

Kelley Family Favorite Green Juice ...12

Orange-Infused Steel-Cut Oats with Blueberries and Almond Slices ...14

Smoked Salmon and Goat Cheese Frittata ...16

Apple, Cinnamon, and Walnut Muffins ...17

Very Blueberry Pancakes ...20

Açai Bowl with Granola, Fruit, and Nuts ...23

Homemade Granola ...24

KELLEY FAMILY FAVORITE GREEN JUICE

This is a *great* way to eat your greens and feel good! My sister and I try to drink a glass every morning. It's sweetened with apples, and the lime and ginger give it a little zing that cuts right through the greens. One of my weekend tasks is to make a big batch of this for the coming week (we freeze what we can't drink that day). If you are looking for ways to feel good all day, drink this!

YIELDS: 1 generous cup, serves 1
TIME: 5 minutes

INGREDIENTS:

3 to 6 cups/450 to 900 g greens, such as spinach, chard, and kale (according to taste)

1 lemon, peeled and quartered

1 (½- to 1-inch/1.5 to 2.5 cm) piece fresh ginger, peeled

2 apples, sliced (including the core/seeds)

spinach

I assume everyone knows spinach is good for you. But do you know why? It's called a superfood for a reason. It's packed with vitamins and fiber, and helps keep your brain sharp. I know I can use that—especially around finals!

DIRECTIONS:

Following the instructions for your juicer, alternate juicing between the greens, lemon, ginger, and apples, so that nothing gets stuck or jammed. Give the juicer enough time to juice before adding more fruit or greens.

To get the most nutrition from your juice, drink it immediately. It will store in the refrigerator for a day, and it's best if you keep it away from the light and exposed to as little air as possible. We use a vacuum sealer with a mason jar attachment to store excess juice in the fridge, or we pour it into a resealable freezer bag, remove as much air as possible, and freeze. The night before you want to drink the juice, remove the bag from the freezer and place in the fridge to thaw.

ORANGE-INFUSED STEEL-CUT OATS WITH BLUEBERRIES AND ALMOND SLICES

Oatmeal is perfect for a chilly day, and it is also a really great power-packed healthy breakfast. This is my all-time favorite oatmeal recipe. Creamy, citrus-y oatmeal, burst of fresh, sweet blueberries, and the nutty crunch from the almonds makes this heaven in your mouth!

YIELDS: **4 servings**
TIME: **30 minutes**

INGREDIENTS:

1 cup/80 g steel-cut oats

2 cups/475 ml freshly squeezed orange juice

1 cup/235 ml unsweetened regular almond milk, or unsweetened vanilla almond milk

¼ teaspoon kosher salt

2 tablespoons pure maple syrup, or to taste

1 pint/340 g fresh blueberries

½ cup/55 g sliced almonds

Orange zest (optional)

DIRECTIONS:

Combine the oats, orange juice, almond milk, and salt with 1 cup/235 ml of water in a saucepan and bring to a boil, then lower the heat to low and bring to a simmer.

Let it simmer, partially covered, for 25 to 30 minutes, or until the liquid is absorbed and the oatmeal is the right chewiness for you. Stir occasionally to keep the oats from sticking to the bottom of the pot.

Add the maple syrup and stir until combined.

Top with fresh blueberries, almonds, and orange zest, if using.

To really take your presentation to the next level, you can serve your oatmeal in an orange peel. Take an orange and cut it in half. Slice a bit of the bottom of the orange "bowl" so that it will stay put and not wobble. Carefully take a paring knife and cut around the inside of the peel, and use your fingers to pull out as much of the orange flesh as possible. Save the orange flesh for eating or juicing, and use the orange peel bowl to serve your oatmeal!

SMOKED SALMON AND GOAT CHEESE FRITTATA

We have great salmon here in the Pacific Northwest, and this is one of my dad's favorite breakfast dishes. Salty salmon and creamy, tangy goat cheese are tucked in a warm frittata with herbs. I made this on Food Network Star Kids . . . and the judges loved it! I know you guys will enjoy it, too. It's the perfect dish for breakfast, brunch, or lunch if you want something easy and packed with flavor.

YIELDS: 4 servings
TIME: 20 minutes

INGREDIENTS:

8 large eggs

1 tablespoon fresh dill, chopped, or 1 teaspoon dried

½ teaspoon kosher salt

¼ teaspoon freshly ground black pepper

2 tablespoons chopped fresh chives

2 ounces/55 g goat cheese

2 ounces/55 g smoked salmon, flaked

2 teaspoons extra-virgin olive oil

DIRECTIONS:

Position a rack in the center of the oven and preheat to 375°F/190°C.

Whisk together the eggs, dill, salt, pepper, and chives in a bowl. Using two spoons or your fingers, separate the goat cheese into small clumps. Fold the goat cheese and salmon into the egg mixture.

Heat the oil in a 10-inch/25.5 cm nonstick, oven-safe skillet over medium-low heat. Pour the egg mixture into the skillet and stir lightly to make sure the filling is evenly distributed in the pan. Cook until the bottom is set but not browned, about 2 minutes. Transfer the skillet to the oven and bake until the center is no longer jiggly and the edges are golden brown, about 8 minutes.

Remove from the oven, cover, and set aside for 5 minutes.

Take a butter knife and run it along the edges of the pan to make sure the frittata isn't sticking, and then slide the frittata onto a large plate. Cut into wedges and serve warm or at room temperature with a simple green salad or sliced tomatoes.

APPLE, CINNAMON, AND WALNUT MUFFINS

This light and fluffy muffin is soft and sweet, with a bit of crunchy cinnamon-sugar sprinkle. I love serving them in easy-to-make rustic muffin liners because they look super cool. These muffins are a perfect choice for brunch and snacks, and I sometimes bring them to school for a class treat—it's always a big hit!

YIELDS: **12 muffins**
TIME: **45 minutes**

INGREDIENTS:

Muffins:

2 cups/260 g white whole wheat flour or 250 g all-purpose flour, divided

1 teaspoon baking soda

¼ teaspoon kosher salt

1 teaspoon ground cinnamon

½ cup/120 ml coconut oil, melted

¾ cup/170 g light brown sugar

¼ cup/85 g honey

2 large eggs

1 cup/245 g unsweetened applesauce (homemade recipe follows)

1 cup/120 g chopped walnuts, toasted

1 cup/150 g grated apple

Topping:

¼ cup/60 g light brown sugar

½ teaspoon ground cinnamon

½ cup/60 g chopped walnuts, toasted

DIRECTIONS:

To make the muffins: Preheat the oven to 350°F/180°C. Line a 12-cup muffin tin with paper liners, or use homemade muffin liners (instructions follow). Combine 1¾ cups/225 g of the flour, baking soda, salt, and cinnamon in a medium bowl.

Whisk the coconut oil, brown sugar, and honey in a large bowl until well combined. Whisk in the eggs and applesauce. Add the dry ingredients and stir just until combined. Stir in the walnuts. Toss the grated apple with the remaining ¼ cup/35 g (25 g if all-purpose) of flour and stir into the batter.

Divide the batter evenly among the prepared muffin cups.

To make the topping: Combine the sugar, cinnamon, and walnuts in a small bowl. Sprinkle on top of the muffins. Bake until puffed and set in the center, about 25 minutes.

homemade applesauce

YIELDS: **about 2 cups/490 g**
TIME: **25 minutes**

INGREDIENTS:

3 medium-size sweet, baking apples, such as Honey Crisp, Pink Lady, or Fuji

1 cinnamon stick

DIRECTIONS:

Peel the apples and core them. Dice the apples into roughly ½-inch/1.5 cm cubes.

Place the apples in a saucepan along with ½ cup/120 ml of water. Add the cinnamon stick. Cover and let it simmer over low heat for 15 to 20 minutes. If it looks too dry, add a bit more water as you cook. If it looks too watery, cook them uncovered to let some water evaporate. Cook until the apples are softened with very little liquid.

Once the apples are cooked, remove the cinnamon stick. Purée the apples in a food processor for a smooth applesauce, or mash them with a potato masher for a chunkier applesauce.

homemade muffin liners

DIRECTIONS:

Cut a 6-inch/15 cm square piece of parchment paper.

Center one square over one of the cups of your muffin tin.

Push the parchment paper into the muffin cup, crease the parchment paper where the edges overlap each other, and insert a narrow glass or juice cup in each muffin cup to keep in place.

When you are ready to scoop your batter into the tin, quickly remove the glass and replace with the batter. These liners look so rustic and cute!

VERY BLUEBERRY PANCAKES

Growing up, my grandma would always make huge batches of blueberry pancakes when I slept over, and my grandpa and I would have pancake-eating contests (I always won, by the way). Blueberry pancakes became one of my favorite breakfast foods and I *love* this recipe! The batter itself has no added sugar, but the blueberries make it perfectly sweet and moist. You don't even need to top it with much maple syrup. This dish brings me lots of good memories.

YIELDS: **8 to 10 pancakes, 4 servings**
TIME: **30 minutes**

INGREDIENTS:

1½ cups/187 g all-purpose flour

½ teaspoon baking powder

Pinch of salt

1 cup/235 ml unsweetened almond milk (or regular milk if you prefer)

1 large egg

2 tablespoons coconut oil, melted

1 teaspoon pure vanilla extract

1 cup/145 g fresh blueberries, or frozen if they are not in season (no need to thaw)

Grapeseed oil for cooking

Pure maple syrup for topping

DIRECTIONS:

Combine the flour, baking powder, and salt in a large bowl.

In a separate bowl, combine the almond milk, egg, coconut oil, and vanilla and mix until smooth.

Pour the wet mixture into the dry mixture and gently stir until there are no remaining lumps.

Fold in the blueberries.

Preheat a nonstick pan over medium heat and grease with a little bit of grapeseed oil.

Pour in ¼ cup/60 ml of batter at a time. When one side is browned, after about 2 minutes, flip and brown the other side, until cooked through.

Top with pure maple syrup and dig in!

blueberries

If you're anything like me, having a healthy complexion is super important. Did you know that blueberries can help with that? These little guys are packed with tons of anti-oxidants, which help to keep your skin healthy. Thank you, blueberries!

AÇAI BOWL WITH GRANOLA, FRUIT, AND NUTS

Açai bowls are a super delicious way to start your morning, and they are gorgeous (totally taking over Instagram)! My version is fruity, tropical, and heavenly, and once it's ready, you won't be able to resist taking a photo! This breakfast is packed with nutrients, vitamins, and antioxidants, and it will give you a ton of energy to start your day.

YIELDS: **1 large or 2 small bowls, 1 to 2 servings**
TIME: **10 minutes**

INGREDIENTS:

1 (3.5-ounce/100 g) packet frozen açai mix (this mix is usually made up of açai, blueberries, and raspberries all blended together and frozen into packets. You can find this in the frozen fruit aisle.)

6 frozen strawberries

½ cup/95 g frozen pineapple

1 tablespoon chia seeds

¾ cup/175 ml freshly squeezed orange juice

Fresh fruit, chopped (I like bananas, strawberries, and blueberries)

Nuts of choice, such as almonds, cashews, or walnuts

Granola (either store-bought or my Homemade Granola [page 24])

Drizzle of honey (I usually add about a tablespoon)

açai berries

Açai berries are not only delicious, but they are also said to be one of the healthiest fruits in the entire world! My all-time favorite benefit of açai is how it boosts your energy. This is why I love having açai for breakfast. It gives me the natural kick-start I need to prepare for a school day. Who needs coffee when you have açai berries?

DIRECTIONS:

In a blender, blend the açai, strawberries, pineapple, chia seeds, and orange juice until smooth. If the açai mixture is too thick, add up to ¼ cup/60 ml of water or more orange juice and blend until creamy and smooth. Scoop it into a bowl.

Top your açai bowl with nuts, granola, and fresh fruit and drizzle with honey to taste. Dig in!

HOMEMADE GRANOLA

Granola is a popular breakfast or snack item, and what I love about my recipe is that it can be super delicious without adding in extra sugar or any artificial ingredients. This granola is made with seeds, oats, and nuts that are kissed with honey and baked until golden brown and heavenly. Top with fresh fruit and some almond milk for a real treat. I like to make a batch ahead of time and store the granola in airtight mason jars, so I always have some ready to munch on.

YIELDS: **8 cups/about 800 g**
TIME: **35 minutes**

INGREDIENTS:

1¾ cups/225 g mixed nuts, such as almonds, cashews, walnuts, etc.

⅔ cup/100 g mixed seeds, such as sunflower, flaxseeds, chia seeds, etc.

5 cups/400 g quick-cooking oats

½ teaspoon pumpkin spice

¾ teaspoon kosher salt

⅓ cup/80 ml grapeseed oil

⅓ cup/115 g honey

2 cups/300 g dried fruit, such as apricots, mangoes, blueberries, strawberries, etc. for serving

Fresh fruit for serving

Unsweetened almond milk for serving

DIRECTIONS:

Preheat the oven to 350°F/180°C.

Put the nuts in a food processor and roughly chop.

Put the chopped nuts into a bowl and add the seeds, oats, pumpkin pie spice, and salt. Mix until combined.

Add the oil and honey, and mix until everything is thoroughly coated.

Spread the mixture on a baking sheet in an even layer.

Bake for 20 to 25 minutes, or until golden brown. Make sure to check on the granola at the 15-minute mark to make sure nothing is burning and to give the baking sheet a little shake to keep everything from sticking to the pan.

Take the granola out of the oven and let it cool. In the meantime, roughly chop the dried fruit.

Pour your granola into a bowl and top with dried fruit and your favorite fresh fruit (mine are blueberries and strawberries).

Pour in the almond milk and enjoy!

my morning routine

I am in no way, shape, or form a morning person. But a good morning routine can turn my bad mood into a good one by the time I have to leave for school. So, I thought I'd share my morning routine to help you start your day on the right foot, while still getting as much sleep as you can.

Prep the Night Before.

The silver lining to not being a morning person is that I'm a night person. That means I have energy the night before to do stuff so I can sleep in as long as possible the next morning. I wish I could even do my hair and makeup the night before . . . but that would get messy. Here's how you can prep the night before to make your mornings run smoother:

LAY OUT YOUR OUTFIT. By doing this, I don't end up wearing sweats and a hoodie every single day! I also make sure I have socks and a sweatshirt next to my bed so I don't have the "it's cold" excuse to stay in bed.

PREP YOUR BREAKFAST. This breakfast section has tons of recipes that can be made ahead of time so you can just grab and go. Try my Homemade Granola, for instance!

PACK YOUR LUNCH. Check out the "Double Duty Dinners" section of this book for tons of recipes that can help you get lunch made the night before.

PACK YOUR BAG. Don't forget that *one* piece of homework you need or that phone charger. It's all ready to go in the morning if you pack it away the night before.

SHOWER. Personally, I like to shower at night. I like going to bed clean, and it also gives my hair a chance to dry overnight so I don't have to spend time in the morning blow-drying it.

Keep It Simple in the Morning.

The more you have to do, the earlier you have to get up. Here's how I simplify my morning:

6AM: WAKE UP. Try not to hit the snooze button.

6:15: EAT BREAKFAST. Hopefully I've prepped something delicious the night before that entices me to get out of bed!

6:30: GET PRESENTABLE.
• Throw on clothes I laid out the night before.
• Wash my face and brush my teeth.
• Do my hair and makeup. I rarely put time into both, so I pick one. Either I do my hair and do bare minimum makeup (or none at all), or I put on some makeup and my hair gets thrown up into a ponytail. I figure if one of those looks good, it will distract from the other.

6:45: EXTRA TIME. I like to give myself just a little bit of wiggle room to keep me from running behind. I usually use the time to finish getting ready or to check social media.

7:00: GRAB AND GO! Get the lunch out of the fridge and grab the bag I packed the night before.

Now by no means am I saying that this morning routine puts me in a good mood *every single morning*, but it totally helps! By having some structure to my routine I'm not as frazzled, and my morning isn't as hectic. Try adding in one or two of these tips, and it might just change your morning, too.

feel-good snacks

So You Can Make It to the Next Meal

I don't know about you guys, but I love snacking. With these recipes, you won't have to feel guilty while you're munching and they will keep you happy and satisfied until your next meal.

CRUNCHY SAVORY
SNACK MIX

You may know I love to play volleyball, and this snack mix is perfect to share with my teammates between games. It's nutty, crunchy, crispy, buttery, and a little tangy . . . it's hard not to eat the whole batch! This is similar to snack mixes you can buy at the store, but I make it with wholesome ingredients so I know exactly what I'm eating.

YIELDS: About 12 cups/860 g, 12 servings
TIME: 1 hour 10 minutes

INGREDIENTS:

6 tablespoons/¾ stick/85 g unsalted butter (or a dairy-free butter alternative)

2 tablespoons Worcestershire sauce

2½ teaspoons seasoning salt

1 teaspoon onion powder

1 teaspoon garlic powder

1 (12.3-ounce/385 g) box multigrain cereal squares

1 cup/30 g spelt pretzels

1 cup/28 g pita chips

1 cup/145 g unsalted almonds

1 cup/140 g unsalted cashews

DIRECTIONS:

Preheat the oven to 250°F/120°C.

Melt the butter in a large roasting pan. Add the Worcestershire sauce, seasoning salt, onion powder, and garlic powder and mix well. Add the rest of the ingredients and mix well, making sure the sauce is coating the mixture evenly.

Spread the mixture evenly in the bottom of the roasting pan and bake for an hour, stirring every 15 minutes or so, until the mixture is golden and crispy and until all moisture from the sauce has evaporated. (Alternatively, if you don't have a large roasting pan, you can melt the butter in a saucepan, add the seasonings, and then thoroughly mix all the ingredients in a big bowl. Spread it out on two baking sheets, and bake as directed.)

Remove from the oven, spread out the mixture on paper towels, and let it cool to room temperature. Store in an airtight container.

GUACAMOLE WITH BAKED TORTILLA CHIPS, 3 WAYS

Guacamole is the ultimate dip. This recipe is my family's all-time favorite because it's creamy with a little zing and so full of flavor! The trick to this guacamole is to pulverize the onion, garlic, and jalapeño so that the flavors can be evenly distributed throughout the guacamole, and you get that awesome flavor in every bite. You'll never buy store-bought guac again!

While you can use the guacamole as a spread on sandwiches or as a dip for veggies, my favorite way to eat guac is with tortilla chips! My tortilla chips are baked, not fried, and they are still ultra-crispy and full of flavor. You can also create cool shapes using different cookie cutters. My favorite is using a bat-shaped cookie cutter for Halloween-themed chips!

Mix things up by making different flavored tortilla chips. The Original Salt chips are a classic and really bring out the corn flavor of the tortilla. The Tangy Lime are my personal favorite, because they are savory and have a nice zing to them. The Spicy Taco chips are dusted with a smoky, savory spice blend, which gives them a perfect little kick. Which one will be your favorite?

guacamole

YIELDS: **2½ cups/225 g**
TIME: **10 minutes**

INGREDIENTS:

1 teaspoon salt, plus more to as needed

3 tablespoons chopped onion

1 teaspoon peeled and minced garlic

1 teaspoon minced jalapeño pepper (or more if you like dip spicy)

3 avocados, peeled, pitted, and diced

3 tablespoons chopped fresh cilantro

2 to 3 tablespoons freshly squeezed lime juice (about 1 big lime)

Large handful of plum tomatoes, chopped

Freshly ground black pepper

DIRECTIONS:

Place the teaspoon of salt and the onion, garlic, and jalapeño in a mortar and pestle or a molcajete (Mexican version of mortar and pestle). Using the pestle, mash until the veggies release all of their juices and resemble a loose paste.

Add the diced avocado, cilantro, and lime juice and mix with a rubber spatula, making sure the paste is evenly distributed among the avocado and everything is combined. Be careful not to mash it completely smooth—you want some texture!

Add the chopped tomato. Mix until combined, being careful not to mash the tomatoes.

Season with salt and black pepper to taste. Serve with tortilla chips or cucumber slices.

baked tortilla chips, 3 ways

YIELDS: **72 chips per version, 6 servings (12 chips per serving)**
TIME: **15 to 20 minutes**

INGREDIENTS:

12 (6-inch/15 cm) corn tortillas (I like to use a combination of various colored tortillas, such as blue corn, whole-grain, etc.)

2 tablespoons grapeseed oil

¼ flavoring of choice (see below)

Original Salt flavoring:

½ teaspoon salt

¼ teaspoon freshly ground black pepper

Tangy Lime flavoring:

¼ cup/60 ml freshly squeezed lime juice

½ teaspoon salt

Spicy Taco flavoring:

½ teaspoon garlic powder

½ teaspoon onion powder

½ teaspoon paprika

1 teaspoon ground cumin

¼ to ½ teaspoon cayenne pepper, to taste

½ teaspoon salt

¼ teaspoon freshly ground black pepper

DIRECTIONS:

Preheat the oven to 350°F/180°C.

Cut out the tortillas into 8 wedges, or into shapes with a cookie cutter of your choice.

Place the tortilla wedges in a single layer on several baking sheets, and brush each side lightly with the grapeseed oil. Season with your flavoring of choice. You'll need to use multiple baking sheets, and depending on the size of your baking sheets, you may have to bake the chips in multiple batches.

For Original Salt and Spicy Taco Chips, bake for 13 to 15 minutes until crispy. For Tangy Lime Chips, bake for 15 to 17 minutes.

Let them cool a bit before you dip them into your guacamole.

avocado

Whether they're in my face mask or on my toast, I absolutely love avocados! They are super delicious, creamy, and insanely good for you. They are full of the healthiest types of fats that our body requires—the types that keep our heart and brain supercharged. Obviously, this is key for not only the teen years, but for all stages of life.

KALE CHIPS, 2 WAYS

Salty, crunchy chips are my ultimate weakness. The issue is, most chips aren't the healthiest choice. Well, these babies totally scratch the itch of having chips without the guilt.

I have the Original Kale Chip recipe for those of you who appreciate the classic. For those who want to take the kale chip up a notch, then you must try the Savory Kale Chips—they are my favorite! They are crispy, nutty, and cheesy, and melt in your mouth. The key ingredient is nutritional yeast, which doesn't sound appetizing, I know, but trust me: it's what adds the intense cheesy flavor that you're gonna love.

original kale chips

YIELDS: **4 cups/55 g**
TIME: **30 minutes**

INGREDIENTS:

About 4 big handfuls of washed and dried kale, torn into bite-size pieces

2 teaspoons grapeseed oil

½ teaspoon sea salt

savory kale chips

YIELDS: **4 cups/55 g**
TIME: **30 minutes**

INGREDIENTS:

About 4 big handfuls of washed kale, torn into bite-size pieces

2 teaspoons grapeseed oil

½ teaspoon sea salt

2 tablespoons nutritional yeast

nutritional yeast

This isn't the kind of yeast you use to bake bread. It's actually used as a seasoning for savory dishes and it adds a fantastic nutty, cheesy flavor. Yes, I know the name "nutritional yeast" doesn't sound appetizing, but it's delicious—plus, it's filled with tons of nutrients, vitamins, and protein, which every growing teen needs.

DIRECTIONS:

Preheat the oven to 350°F/180°C. Line two baking sheets with parchment paper.

Combine the ingredients in a bowl and massage the kale until every leaf is coated evenly.

Spread the kale evenly in a single layer on the baking sheets and bake for 12 to 20 minutes, or until leaves are crisp but not brown (brown kale chips are bitter!), checking at 12 minutes, and again every 2 minutes after that.

FRONANAS: FROZEN PEANUT BUTTER AND CHOCOLATE BANANA SANDWICHES

These are perfect little treats for after school. It's the ultimate combo: peanut butter, banana, and a bit of chocolate. These are so easy, and they're one of the first things my sister and I ever made on our own to practice "knife skills" with a butter knife. We named these "Fronanas" (short for Frozen Bananas) and it's stuck at our house ever since.

YIELDS: **12 pieces**
TIME: **5 minutes (plus freezing time)**

INGREDIENTS:

1 banana

2 tablespoons peanut butter (we use 100% Valencia peanut butter)

⅓ cup/60 g semisweet or dark chocolate chips

DIRECTIONS:

Peel the banana and trim the ends. Cut the banana crosswise into ¼-inch/6 mm slices.

Spread half of the slices with ½ teaspoon of peanut butter apiece and top each with one of the remaining slices of banana to form a "sandwich."

Melt the chocolate chips in the microwave on HIGH, stirring every 15 seconds until smooth, 1 to 2 minutes. Spread a dollop of chocolate over the top of each Fronana. It looks especially cool if you let some of the chocolate drizzle down the side. Freeze until firm.

CHOCOLATE PEANUT BUTTER SOFT-SERVE WITH BERRIES

I am a sucker for chocolate and peanut butter, so this soft-serve is perfect for me. It's velvety, rich, and super creamy. A bonus is that it's dairy-free, which I love because dairy makes my skin break out. It's just as good as regular ice cream, but I can eat all I want and still have clear skin—hallelujah! You won't believe how good this is!

YIELDS: **2 large or 4 small servings**
TIME: **5 minutes**

INGREDIENTS:

2 very ripe bananas, frozen

½ to ¾ cup/120 to 175 ml unsweetened almond milk

2 tablespoons cacao powder

¼ cup/65 g peanut butter

Pinch of sea salt

1 teaspoon pure vanilla extract

Fresh berries of your choice

DIRECTIONS:

Place the bananas, ½ cup/120 ml of the almond milk, and the cacao powder, peanut butter, sea salt, and vanilla in a blender and blend until smooth. If needed, add more almond milk, a little bit at a time, until smooth. Be careful not to add too much milk or it will turn into a milk shake (which is just as good, so it's really not a problem).

Pour into a glass and top with your favorite berries.

ZUCCHINI PUFFS

These are lighter than traditional zucchini bread and make a great snack. They are sweet, fluffy, and come in a perfect little size. My family always makes a huge batch and pops them in the freezer so that way we can just take one out whenever we are hungry. My sister and I are addicted to these because they are such an easy and delicious snack that we can get after school or for breakfast.

YIELDS: **16**
TIME: **35 minutes**

INGREDIENTS:

½ cup/1 stick/113 g unsalted butter (or a dairy-free butter alternative)

¾ cup/255 g honey

1 large egg

2 cups/260 g whole wheat flour

1 teaspoon baking soda

½ teaspoon ground cinnamon

Pinch of freshly grated nutmeg

Pinch of ground cloves

Pinch of salt

1 cup/80 g old-fashioned rolled oats

1 cup/145 g raisins

1 cup/120 g grated zucchini

DIRECTIONS:

Preheat the oven to 375°F/190°C. Line a cookie sheet with parchment paper.

Cream the butter and honey with an electric mixer or by hand. Add the egg and beat well.

Combine the flour, baking soda, cinnamon, nutmeg, cloves, salt, rolled oats, and raisins in a separate bowl.

Add the flour mixture to the butter mixture and mix until fully combined. Stir in the zucchini.

Scoop little tablespoon-size balls of the batter onto the prepared cookie sheet, placing them 1 inch/2.5 cm apart.

Bake for 10 to 15 minutes (time may vary as all ovens are different).

Transfer to a cooling rack and let cool. Place any you want to eat later into a resealable plastic bag and freeze.

PEACH AND
OAT BARS

These bars are my go-to treat to bring to school to share with teachers and friends. You have a golden, buttery, sweet granola base topped with a sweet and tart peach jam and chewy dried peaches—but you can customize it with your favorite fruit. These bars are a healthier option to bring to school parties rather than the typical donuts, cupcakes, and other store-bought treats. And trust me, my friends totally approve!

YIELDS: **12 bars**
TIME: **55 minutes (20 minutes prep, 35 baking)**

INGREDIENTS:

Grapeseed oil for baking dish

1¾ cups/219 g all-purpose flour

¾ cup/170 g packed light
brown sugar

1 teaspoon ground cinnamon

¾ teaspoon fine sea salt

¾ teaspoon baking soda

1¾ cups/140 g old-fashioned
rolled oats

1 cup/2 sticks/225 g unsalted
butter, melted (or a dairy-free
butter alternative)

1 large egg, at room
temperature, beaten

1 teaspoon pure vanilla extract

1¼ cups/400 g peach jam
(or your favorite flavor jam)

½ cup/65 g dried peaches,
chopped into small pieces
(or your favorite dried fruit)

DIRECTIONS:

Preheat the oven to 350°F/180°C.

Oil a 13 x 9 x 2-inch/33 x 23 x 5 cm baking dish, and place parchment paper inside so the far ends overhang the sides (this will make it easier to remove the baked bars. Press the parchment paper down, so it sticks to the oiled dish.

In a large bowl, mix together the flour, brown sugar, cinnamon, salt, and baking soda until thoroughly combined. Stir in the oats.

Add the butter, egg, and vanilla and stir until everything is well combined.

In a separate small bowl, mix together the jam and dried fruit.

Using your hands, lightly press ¾ of the oat mixture onto the bottom of the prepared pan in an even layer.

Spread the jam mixture evenly over the oat mixture, leaving a ½-inch/1.5 cm border around the edge of the pan.

Crumble the remaining oat mixture over the jam. Bake until light golden, 30 to 35 minutes. Remove from the oven and let cool completely.

Cut the bars into small rectangles and store in an airtight container for up to 3 days.

KALAMATA CHICKPEA DIP WITH CRUDITÉS AND HOMEMADE PITA CHIPS

I don't want to brag, but I really do think this is the best chickpea dip ever! I've been asked for the recipe so many times, and have also been asked to bring it to parties, that I now end up making it at least once a month. The main difference between this dip and hummus is that I omit the traditional tahini (sesame paste) and add enough lemon and olive oil to make it extra-creamy and smooth. If you try it, you'll see why it's become famous among our family and friends!

chickpea dip

YIELDS: **About 4 cups/984 g, 10 to 12 servings**
TIME: **10 minutes**

INGREDIENTS:

1 garlic clove, peeled

2 (15-ounce/425 g) cans chickpeas, drained and rinsed

Juice of 1½ lemons

1 teaspoon salt

¼ teaspoon freshly ground black pepper

½ cup/120 ml extra-virgin olive oil

¼ cup/25 g Kalamata olives, pits removed

Additional salt and freshly ground pepper to taste

DIRECTIONS:

In a food processor, process the garlic to chop it up.

Add the chickpeas, lemon juice, salt, and pepper and purée until smooth.

While the processor is running, slowly drizzle in the olive oil, scraping the sides of the bowl at least once. Make sure your dip isn't too thick. You can add more olive oil or lemon to make it loose and creamy.

Add the Kalamata olives and pulse in the food processor about 8 times, just enough so that they are broken up into chunks.

Season with salt and pepper to taste. Use a rubber spatula to thoroughly mix the olives into the dip and transfer to a serving bowl. Serve with crudités (fancy word for veggie sticks) and Homemade Pita Chips (recipe follows).

homemade pita chips

YIELDS: **8 servings**
TIME: **10 minutes**

INGREDIENTS:

6 pita bread pockets

2 tablespoons grapeseed oil

Salt and freshly ground black pepper

DIRECTIONS:

Preheat the oven to 400°F/200°C.

Separate the pita pockets into two thin circles apiece, and lightly brush a thin layer of oil on both sides of each circle of bread.

Cut each circle into 8 wedges and place the wedges on a baking sheet in a single layer (you will have to use more than one baking sheet).

Lightly sprinkle the wedges with salt and pepper to taste.

Bake for 7 minutes, or until golden brown and crispy.

TIP

taming the snack attack

There are times when, all of a sudden, I'll realize that I'm starving, and if I don't have something to eat *now*, I'm going to die. For me, those are the times when I tend to grab whatever is in front of me, even if it's not a great choice (or even something I really want). Here are some of my strategies for taming the Snack Attack:

BYOS. Or, Bring Your Own Snack. I like to always keep raw almonds or dried fruit in my bag. That way, I always have a healthier option on hand if I'm suddenly famished.

DRINK UP. Sometimes when you think you're hungry, you're actually just dehydrated. So, the next time you have a Snack Attack, get a drink of water and take a moment to see whether you were just thirsty.

STICK TO WHOLE FOODS. Fresh, raw snacks are way better for you than prepackaged foods because they still have all their nutrients and fiber. Whether it's an apple or some almonds, whole food snacks will help keep you satisfied until your next meal.

CREATE AN ANYTIME DRAWER. In my house, we call the very bottom drawer in our fridge the "Anytime Drawer." It's always filled with nuts, fruits, vegetables, and other healthy snacks. We have full access to this drawer whenever we want, so it's super convenient and a really great way to make sure you're eating fresh foods without having to think too much about it. It's especially good for little kids, because they can take whatever they want without having to ask, and it gives them a sense of freedom and choice.

PUT IT IN A BOWL. If you're just eating straight out of a bag or box, you won't be paying as much attention to how much you're eating and you will end up endlessly snacking. If you put the snack in a separate small bowl, you will be more aware of the foods you are eating and enjoy them more without overdoing it.

feel-good snacks

double-duty weeknight dinners

Make Enough for Leftovers— You'll Want to Pack It for Lunch

Making school lunches from scratch in the morning is a pain in the butt! My double-duty weeknight dinners are either great as leftovers the next day or they can transform into a new and improved meal that you can easily take to school without all the fuss of cooking from scratch when you are rushing out the door.

DINNER TRANSFORMS INTO LUNCH

STARTS AS:

THAI-INSPIRED GRILLED BEEF SALAD

This salad is one of our family favorites, and my sister is known for wanting this all the time. The juicy beef with the fresh veggies tossed in a savory-tangy dressing is amazing. I always make a giant batch, enough for leftovers.

YIELDS: **4 servings + leftovers**
TIME: **45 minutes active + marinating time**

INGREDIENTS:

Steak:

2 pounds/905 g flank steak, 1 to 1½ inches/2.5 to 4 cm thick

"Dressenade" (what I call dressing + marinade):

1 cup/235 ml freshly squeezed lime juice

1¼ cups/285 ml low-sodium soy sauce

1¼ cups/285 ml grapeseed oil

¾ cup/179 g light brown sugar

3 large garlic cloves, peeled and pressed (about 1½ tablespoons)

1 tablespoon grated fresh ginger

¼ cup/65 g creamy peanut butter

Salad:

1 head romaine lettuce, torn (about 4½ cups/248 g)

1 head red leaf lettuce, torn (about 4½ cups/248 g)

1 medium-size shallot, thinly sliced into half-moons and soaked in water (to remove its bite)

¾ cup/30 g fresh cilantro leaves, rinsed and dried

1½ cups/60 g fresh basil leaves, sliced into thin ribbons

1¼ cups/169 g cucumber that has been cut into matchsticks

¾ cup/83 g carrot, cut into thin ribbons with a potato peeler

1 (8.8-ounce/249 g) package rice vermicelli or rick stick noodles, prepared according to package instructions, drained, and chilled

DIRECTIONS:

Pat the meat dry. Place in a resealable plastic bag.

In a medium bowl, combine all the dressenade ingredients, except the peanut butter.

Pour ⅓ of the mixture into the bag with the meat. Seal tightly, getting as much air out of the bag as possible, and marinate in the refrigerator for at least 4 hours or overnight, turning occasionally.

Pour the remaining ⅔ of the dressenade mixture into a blender or food processor. Add the peanut butter and blend until smooth. Store the dressenade in the fridge. Half will be used to dress the salad, and the other half will be used in tomorrow's lunch.

Oil your grill or grill pan and preheat. Grill the steak until medium-rare (about 8 minutes per side). Let it rest for at least 10 to 20 minutes, then slice thinly against the grain. Set aside about ½ pound/115 g of the steak for tomorrow's lunch (enough for 8 spring rolls).

Prepare the salad: Combine ⅔ each of the lettuce, sliced shallot, cilantro, basil, cucumber, carrot, and noodles in a salad bowl. The remaining ⅓ of the salad ingredients will be used for tomorrow's lunch.

Add ½ of the dressenade from your fridge and toss to coat. Divide the salad among 4 plates and top with the sliced steak.

TURNS INTO:

STEAK SPRING ROLLS WITH SRIRACHA MAYO AND SOY-LIME DIPPING SAUCE

The previous salad transforms into the most delicious spring rolls ever! All of the same delicious flavors of the salad, along with a creamy, spicy sriracha mayo, are wrapped tight with silky rice noodles and served with a tangy dipping sauce . . . oh, YES!

YIELDS: **8 rolls, 4 servings**
TIME: **30 minutes**

INGREDIENTS:

From the night before:

Dressenade

Romaine lettuce, red leaf lettuce, shallot, cilantro, basil, cucumber, and carrot

Sliced flank steak

New ingredients:

6 tablespoons mayonnaise

2 tablespoons Sriracha sauce

1 teaspoon freshly squeezed lime juice

¼ teaspoon soy sauce

8 rice paper wrappers

DIRECTIONS:

Take the leftover dressenade from last night and add a tablespoon of water. Refrigerate until ready to use.

To make the sriracha mayo, combine the mayonnaise, Sriracha, lime juice, and soy sauce in a bowl and mix well. If you have a squeeze bottle, put the sriracha mayo in the squeeze bottle and refrigerate until your spring rolls are ready to assemble.

To assemble the spring rolls, take a sauté pan or plate and fill with enough cold water to submerge the rice paper (about ¼ inch/6 mm). Slide a sheet of rice paper in the water and leave it there for 10 to 15 seconds. Remove the paper, place it on a plate or cutting board, and dab off any excess water with a paper towel.

Think of the spring roll as a burrito. In the bottom third of the paper (closest to you), place some vermicelli, veggies, and herbs. Squeeze some sriracha mayo on top of the filling, then add a strip or two of steak. Bring the lower edge up over the filling, fold in the two side flaps, and then roll the entire thing up, rolling away from you.

Continue making spring rolls until you have used up the ingredients. Serve with the dipping sauce and extra sriracha mayo on the side. If you are making the spring rolls the night before, cover the rolls with a damp paper towel, wrap tightly in plastic wrap, and refrigerate overnight. Be sure the spring rolls aren't touching because they will stick together!

START AS:

GRILLED FLANK STEAK
AND VEGGIES

Juicy, tangy steak with sweet, smoky veggies—it's the perfect combo! This is one of our family's go-to dishes because it's a real crowd pleaser. The steak and veggies are both grilled on the barbecue, which makes for easy cooking and easy cleanup. Add some crusty bread and a colorful crispy green salad, and you've got a scrumptious meal.

YIELDS: **4 servings + leftovers**
TIME: **45 minutes active + marinating time**

INGREDIENTS:

Steak:

¾ cup/175 ml grapeseed oil

½ cup/120 ml soy sauce

6 tablespoons red wine vinegar

3 tablespoons freshly squeezed lemon juice

2 tablespoons plus 1 teaspoon Worcestershire sauce

1½ tablespoons Dijon mustard

3 garlic cloves, peeled and pressed

¾ teaspoon freshly ground black pepper

2 pounds/905 g flank steak

Grilled Veggies:

About 4 of each of your favorite veggies, such as zucchini, bell peppers, beets, and onions

Grapeseed oil

Salt and freshly ground black pepper

DIRECTIONS:

Prepare the steak: Place the oil, soy sauce, vinegar, lemon juice, Worcestershire sauce, mustard, garlic, and black pepper in a resealable plastic bag. Seal and mix well.

Place the steak into the bag and seal, getting as much air out as possible. Refrigerate for 6 hours or overnight.

Prep your veggies for grilling: Quarter the zucchini lengthwise, seed and quarter the peppers, peel and slice the beets, and peel and slice the onions into rings. Place each kind of vegetable into a separate resealable plastic bag and add just enough grapeseed oil to each to coat.

Preheat the grill to medium-high heat. Oil the grill. Grill the steak for 8 minutes per side for medium-rare. Set the steak aside and let it rest.

Place the vegetables on the grill, sprinkle with salt and black pepper to taste, and grill until tender and caramelized. The time will depend on the hardness of the vegetable (beets will take much longer than zucchini, for example). Set aside ¼ of the veggies for tomorrow's lunch.

Slice the steak, and set aside ¼ of it for tomorrow's lunch. Serve the remaining steak with the veggies, some crusty bread, and a crispy green salad.

TURNS INTO:

EASY STEAK AND VEGGIE WRAP WITH CAPER DILL CREAM

I love a good steak wrap, and this recipe is no exception. My wrap is packed with tender steak, fresh veggies, and a killer herb sour cream for some tang. It's amazing. But do you want to know the best part? You'll be using last night's leftovers to create this dish for lunch!

YIELDS: **4 servings**
TIME: **10 minutes**

INGREDIENTS:

From the night before:

Grilled and sliced flank steak

Grilled vegetables

New ingredients:

½ cup/115 g sour cream

2 tablespoons mayonnaise

1 tablespoon chopped capers

1½ teaspoons chopped fresh dill

1½ teaspoons freshly squeezed lemon juice

Salt and freshly ground black pepper

4 flour tortillas

2 cups/110 g shredded romaine lettuce

1 cup/150 g halved cherry tomatoes, halved

DIRECTIONS:

Mix together the sour cream, mayonnaise, capers, dill, lemon, and salt and pepper to taste in a small bowl.

Spread some of the sour cream mixture on a tortilla. Add some lettuce, pieces of steak, grilled veggies, and tomatoes.

Roll up the tortilla like a burrito. Stick in a toothpick to help keep it together. Repeat to create the remaining 3 wraps.

GRILLED WHOLE CHICKEN WITH CILANTRO CHIMICHURRI AND GARLIC-LEMON BROCCOLETTE

You *must* make this Cilantro Chimichurri! It's tangy, garlicky, and bursting with flavor. My family puts a twist on the classic Argentinian chimichurri and uses all cilantro instead of adding parsley—and it's amazing! My mom can never get enough; we tease her for spooning more and more on her plate, but I can't blame her.

This sauce is versatile. You can dip breads and veggies—whatever you want—but my favorite is with grilled chicken. Grilling the chicken whole is an easy way to get moist, smoky, and flavorful chicken without a bunch of work.

The garlicky, lemony broccolette (also called broccolini) can be made on the same grill as soon as the chicken comes off. Add something fresh like a simple green salad or sliced tomatoes with a sprinkle of salt and olive oil for a nice family meal.

YIELDS: **4 servings + leftovers**
TIME: **30 minutes prep (15 for chimichurri, 15 for chicken)**
    and 45 minutes to grill chicken

chimichurri sauce

INGREDIENTS:

4 garlic cloves, peeled

2 cups/90 g fresh cilantro leaves and stems

¼ cup/60 ml freshly squeezed lemon juice

1½ teaspoons salt

1 teaspoon red pepper flakes

3 tablespoons onion, chopped

1½ tablespoons red wine vinegar

1 cup/235 ml extra-virgin olive oil

DIRECTIONS:

Place the garlic in a food processor and chop finely.

Scrape down the sides and add all the remaining ingredients, except the oil. Pulse together.

While the food processor is running, slowly add the olive oil, scraping down the sides of the food processor as needed, until the sauce is smooth.

Refrigerate until ready for use. Set aside 1 cup/235 ml of the sauce for tomorrow's lunch.

grilled whole chicken

INGREDIENTS:

1 whole chicken (4 to 6 pounds/ 1.8 to 2.7 kg)	2 teaspoons freshly ground black pepper
4 to 6 garlic cloves, peeled and pressed	2 teaspoons lemon zest
1 tablespoon salt	1 tablespoon grapeseed oil

DIRECTIONS:

Heat your grill on a medium-high heat.

Remove the chicken from the refrigerator. Use sharp kitchen scissors to spatchcock the chicken. To do this, place the chicken breast-side down and cut along one side of the backbone, then the other side, to remove it. Flip the chicken over, and firmly press on the breastbone to flatten it out. This will allow the chicken to cook evenly.

Mix together the garlic, salt, pepper, and lemon zest in a small bowl.

Rub the chicken with the oil and then rub with the garlic mixture. Place the chicken, breast-side down, on the grill. Cover the grill and cook for 5 to 7 minutes, until the breast is golden brown and crispy.

Flip the chicken over and continue to cook until the underside of the chicken starts to brown, 10 to 20 minutes.

Turn off all the burners and cover the grill. Then, continue to cook until the bird is cooked through, 10 to 25 minutes longer. It is done when the thickest part of the breast reads 155°F/68°C on a meat thermometer.

Place the chicken on a cutting board and tent it with foil to let it rest. Prepare the Grilled Garlic-Lemon Broccolette (recipe follows).

Cut up your chicken into 8 pieces (2 thighs, 2 legs, and cut each breast in half) and set aside two big pieces for tomorrow's salad.

Bring the chimichurri sauce out of the refrigerator and let it come to room temperature. Give it a stir. Plate the remaining chicken, and drizzle with the chimichurri sauce. Pour some additional chimichurri into a small bowl so guests (like my mom) can drizzle more as they eat. Serve with the Garlic-Lemon Broccolette.

garlic-lemon broccolette

YIELDS: **4 servings + leftovers**
TIME: **20 minutes**

INGREDIENTS:

2 pounds/900 g broccolette

¼ cup/60 ml grapeseed oil

3 garlic cloves, peeled and pressed

Salt and freshly ground black pepper

½ large lemon, plus lemon slices for garnish

DIRECTIONS:

Trim the tough ends of the broccolette.

In a bowl, toss with the oil, pressed garlic, and salt and pepper to taste.

Once the chicken comes off the grill, place the broccolette on the grill.

Grill for about 8 minutes on each side over medium-high heat, until the broccolette is tender and has some grill marks.

Arrange on a serving dish, squeeze the juice from the ½ lemon over the top, and garnish with lemon slices.

CHICKEN CHIMICHURRI QUINOA SALAD

I love quinoa, and when I pair it with my family's favorite chimichurri sauce, magic happens! This quinoa salad is fluffy, with bits of creamy avocado, sweet fresh tomatoes, juicy chicken, and a killer sauce that gives it a nice kick. The textures and flavors are insane!

YIELDS: 4 servings
TIME: 25 minutes

INGREDIENTS:

From the night before:

Grilled chicken

½ to 1 cup/120 to 235 ml chimichurri sauce

Broccolette

New ingredients:

1 cup/173 g uncooked quinoa

2 cups/475 ml chicken stock

½ cup/75 g halved cherry tomatoes, halved

1 avocado, peeled, pitted, and diced

Handful of fresh cilantro, chopped

DIRECTIONS:

Wash the quinoa and let it drip-dry.

Place the quinoa in a pot along with the chicken stock. Bring it to a boil, put the lid on, and let simmer for 15 minutes. Remove from the heat, let cool for 5 minutes, then fluff it up with a fork.

Shred last night's chicken into bite-size pieces, discarding the skin and bones. You should have about 2 cups/280 g.

Chop the broccolette into bite-size pieces. Add the chopped broccolette, tomatoes, avocado, chicken, and ½ cup/120 ml of chimichurri sauce to the quinoa, and mix well. Taste, and add more chimichurri sauce as needed.

Sprinkle the chopped cilantro on top.

If you are making this for a school lunch, refrigerate overnight and pack with an ice pack to keep the chicken in the salad cool until lunchtime.

HAPPY LEFTOVERS

The most common dish you will find in my lunchbox is leftovers from the night before. One, because it's easy; and two, because I usually love the food I had yesterday for dinner so much that I want to eat it again. Here are some of my all-time favorite dinners that are perfect to take to school the next day. Trust me: you're going to want to eat these two days in a row!

TERIYAKI CHICKEN LETTUCE WRAPS WITH QUICK PICKLES AND MISO DRIZZLE

This dish is special to me, because it was the reason I was able to meet my idol, Jamie Oliver. I entered his worldwide recipe video contest, and although I didn't win, he was impressed and asked me to be part of his Food Tube Network, a group of amazing chefs who collaborate and share recipes on his YouTube channel.

These lettuce wraps are fresh and filled with savory, tender chicken, sweet carrots, salty, crunchy cucumbers, and an earthy miso drizzle. If you want to take leftovers for lunch, keep them in the fridge overnight and add ice packs to your lunch bag in the morning to make sure everything stays fresh.

YIELDS: **4 to 6 servings (4 with leftovers for lunch)**

TIME: **30 minutes active + marinating**

INGREDIENTS:

8 to 10 boneless, skinless chicken thighs (2 to 2½ pounds/905 g to 1.1 kg)

2 cups/475 ml store-bought teriyaki sauce

Grapeseed oil for grill

2 large heads Bibb lettuce, washed, dried, and leaves separated

1 large carrot, cut into thin ribbons with a potato peeler

1 recipe Quick Pickles (recipe follows)

1 recipe Miso Drizzle (recipe follows)

DIRECTIONS:

Place the chicken in a large resealable plastic bag. Pour in the teriyaki sauce. Seal the bag, squeezing out as much air as possible. Give it a good shake to ensure that all the chicken is coated evenly. Transfer to the refrigerator and marinate for at least 4 hours or overnight.

Preheat a grill to medium-high. Oil the grill grates. Remove the chicken from the bag and discard any extra marinade. Grill the chicken until lightly charred and cooked through, 4 to 5 minutes per side. Let the chicken rest for about 10 minutes, then slice the chicken.

To assemble the wraps, stack 2 Bibb lettuce leaves together to make a cup. Fill with a few slices of chicken, several ribbons of carrot, and a few Quick Pickles. Spoon a little bit of the Miso Drizzle over the top.

To take for lunch, pack all the ingredients separately and assemble right before eating.

quick pickles

INGREDIENTS:

1 medium-size English cucumber, sliced crosswise on a mandoline into paper-thin rounds

1 teaspoon kosher salt

DIRECTIONS:

Place the cucumbers in a colander set over a large bowl. Sprinkle with the salt and toss to coat. Set aside for 30 minutes. Squeeze as much as the moisture out as you can with your hands.

miso drizzle

INGREDIENTS:

2 tablespoons red miso paste

2 teaspoons freshly squeezed lemon juice

1 teaspoon soy sauce or tamari

DIRECTIONS:

Combine the miso paste, lemon juice, soy sauce, and 2 tablespoons of water in a small bowl and stir until smooth.

OVERNIGHT GINGER-SOY CHICKEN

For me, the key to some of my favorite meat dishes is the marinade. You all probably know that the longer you let something marinate, the more flavor it absorbs. Well, for this recipe, the chicken marinates for a whole 24 hours—that's a whole lot of flavor! This chicken is a little sweet from the honey and savory from the soy sauce, garlic, and ginger. Big flavor goes all the way from skin to bone, and it is so delicious! You won't believe how easy it is.

YIELDS: **4 to 6 servings (4 with leftovers for lunch)**
TIME: **45 minutes + marinating**

INGREDIENTS:

½ cup/120 ml soy sauce

5 tablespoons honey

3 tablespoons grated fresh ginger

1 tablespoon peeled and minced garlic, or peeled and pressed through a garlic press

2 teaspoons toasted sesame oil

1 teaspoon freshly ground black pepper

3 to 4 pounds/1.4 to 1.8 kg skin-on, bone-in drumsticks and thighs

Green onions, chopped, for garnish

DIRECTIONS:

Combine the soy sauce, honey, ginger, garlic, sesame oil, and pepper in a bowl.

Place the chicken pieces in a big resealable bag and pour in the marinade. Get as much air out as possible and seal. Place the bag in the refrigerator for about 24 hours, turning once or twice so the marinade can seep into all the chicken.

When you are ready to bake the chicken, preheat the oven to 475°F/240°C. Take the chicken out of the refrigerator and place it, skin-side up, in an ovenproof baking dish (4 pounds/1.8 kg of chicken should just fit into a 13 x 9-inch/33 x 23 cm dish).

Pour the leftover marinade from the bag over the chicken into the baking dish.

Bake for 30 to 40 minutes, until the chicken is cooked through and the skin becomes brown and crispy. If the skin isn't browned by the time the chicken is cooked through, turn the broiler on for a few minutes to crisp up the skin.

Transfer the chicken to a platter. Garnish with green onions and serve with brown rice. The Garlic-Lemon Broccolette (page 60) is a perfect side dish.

To take for lunch, pack your chicken in a container and keep it in the fridge overnight. All you have to do in the morning is grab your container, an ice pack to keep your chicken cool until lunch, a napkin, and a fork, and you're good to go!

ginger

Ginger is a key flavor in many of the dishes I love to make. You have probably used it for its earthy, spicy flavor, but did you know that ginger is amazingly good for you, too? It strengthens your immune system, and it helps your body fight to keep sickness at bay, so you can focus on the important stuff, like **having fun**.

MOROCCAN-SPICED MEAT SAUCE WITH GOAT CHEESE

Moroccan pasta is one of my favorite meals ever! Whenever my mom asks Lexi or me what we want for dinner, this is usually what we ask for first. The spicy meat sauce with a hint of cinnamon and creamy goat cheese is just *so* delicious. The spinach adds heartiness and soaks up all the amazing flavor from the sauce. I have made this for many of my friends and they always rave about it!

YIELDS: **4 servings over pasta**
TIME: **20 minutes**

INGREDIENTS:

1 tablespoon grapeseed oil

½ small onion, chopped (about ½ cup/80 g)

1 garlic clove, peeled and pressed

1 pound/455 g lean ground beef

2 teaspoons ground cumin

2 teaspoons paprika

½ teaspoon ground ginger

½ teaspoon ground cinnamon

¼ teaspoon cayenne pepper

3 cups/735 g plain tomato-based pasta sauce

12 ounces/340 g dried spaghetti, or your favorite pasta

4 cups/120 g fresh organic baby spinach

Salt and freshly ground black pepper

¼ cup/38 g crumbled goat cheese

DIRECTIONS:

Place the oil in a large saucepan and heat over medium heat. Sauté the onion and garlic until the onion is translucent, about 5 minutes. Add the beef and cook until browned and crumbly.

Add the cumin, paprika, ginger, cinnamon, and cayenne. Stir until evenly mixed. Pour in the pasta sauce and simmer over medium-low heat for about 15 minutes.

While the pasta sauce is simmering, cook the pasta according to the instructions on the package. Drain the pasta.

Put all the spinach into the pasta sauce and keep stirring until the leaves are wilted. Season with salt and black pepper to taste. Top the pasta with the meat sauce and sprinkle with small chunks of goat cheese.

To take to lunch, pack your leftover pasta and sauce in a container, the goat cheese in a separate container, and store in the fridge. The next morning, pack the containers with an ice pack and a fork. You can eat it at room temperature or warm it up in a microwave. Sprinkle on the goat cheese, and enjoy.

KALE, QUINOA, AND AVOCADO SALAD WITH DIJON VINAIGRETTE

Many people assume that kale tastes bad or boring because it's one of the healthiest foods on the planet. I'm going to prove them all wrong! This salad is *amazing*. Creamy avocado, sweet tomato, and tangy lemon cling to the kale, which softens from all the juices. The kale and quinoa also soak up the flavors and make this hearty enough to eat as a main meal. Also, can we take a moment to appreciate all the colors?

YIELDS: **4 to 6 servings (4 as a main, 6 as a side)**
TIME: **30 minutes**

INGREDIENTS:

1 cup/173 g uncooked quinoa

2 cups/475 ml chicken or vegetable stock

½ cup/120 ml freshly squeezed lemon juice

1 teaspoon Dijon mustard

1 tablespoon nutritional yeast

½ cup/120 ml extra-virgin olive oil

Salt and freshly ground black pepper

1½ to 2 bunches curly kale

2 small or 1 large avocado

1 pint/275 g plum tomatoes, in a variety of colors

quinoa

Quinoa (pronounced "keen-wah") is a healthy grain with a funky name. It is delicious and I love it in salads or as a side for meats and fish. I bet you didn't know that quinoa has twice as much fiber as other grains, which is super helpful for cleaning out your system.

DIRECTIONS:

Rinse the quinoa and combine it with the stock in a pot. Bring to a boil, lower the heat to low, cover, and simmer until the quinoa is tender, about 15 minutes. Turn off the heat and let sit for 5 minutes.

Meanwhile, to make the dressing, combine the lemon juice, mustard, and nutritional yeast in a bowl. Slowly drizzle in the oil while whisking to emulsify the dressing and make it creamy. Add salt and pepper to taste.

Wash and stem the kale. You can do this by holding the stem with one hand and running the other hand down the stem from base to tip, ripping off the leaf in the process. Tear into bite-size pieces and place in a large bowl.

Once the quinoa has cooled enough to handle, add it to the kale.

Pour half of the dressing over the kale salad and mix to coat, using clean hands or two wooden spoons. Add more dressing as needed.

Peel and pit the avocado and cut into bite-size pieces. Halve the tomatoes. Reserve some of the tomatoes for garnish, and carefully fold the rest along with the avocado in with the kale and quinoa.

Pile the salad onto a large serving platter and top with the reserved tomatoes.

Pack any leftover quinoa salad in a container and keep it in the fridge. The next day, grab the quinoa salad, a fork, and a napkin, and you are good to go!

ROASTED VEGGIE AND QUINOA SALAD WITH FETA, BASIL, AND PINE NUTS

If you can't tell by now, I'm a big fan of quinoa! This dish is by far the most popular side dish of our entire family. My mom and I always double or triple the recipe just so we can have enough for leftovers, because it tastes even better the next day—it's got such good flavor. The roasted veggies are caramelized, the quinoa is fluffy and soaks up all the citrus vinaigrette, and the feta adds a creamy, tangy element.

YIELDS: **4 to 6 servings (4 as a main, 6 as a side)**
TIME: **45 minutes**

INGREDIENTS:

1 small eggplant, peeled and ¾-inch/2 cm diced

1 red bell pepper, seeded and 1-inch/2.5 cm diced

1 yellow bell pepper, seeded and 1-inch/2.5 cm diced

1 red onion, peeled and 1-inch/2.5 cm diced

2 garlic cloves, peeled and pressed

⅓ cup/80 ml grapeseed oil

1½ teaspoons kosher salt

½ teaspoon freshly ground black pepper

1 cup/173 g uncooked quinoa

2 cups/475 ml vegetable or chicken stock

Dressing:

⅓ cup/80 ml freshly squeezed lemon juice (from about 2 lemons)

⅓ cup/80 ml olive oil

1 teaspoon kosher salt

½ teaspoon freshly ground black pepper

Toppings:

4 green onions, minced

¼ cup/35 g pine nuts, toasted

15 fresh basil leaves, sliced into thin ribbons, plus a few more for garnish

⅓ cup/50 g feta cheese for sprinkling on top

DIRECTIONS:

Preheat the oven to 425°F/220°C.

Toss the eggplant, bell peppers, onion, and garlic with the oil, salt, and black pepper in a large bowl. Pour onto a large sheet pan, spreading out the veggies into one thin, even layer (use two sheet pans if needed so the vegetables are not crowded). Roast for 25 to 30 minutes, until soft and browned on the edges, turning once with a spatula.

Place the quinoa and stock in a saucepan. Bring to a boil and then lower the heat to low and bring to simmer. Cover and let cook for 15 minutes. Turn off the heat and let the quinoa sit for another 5 minutes. Then fluff it with a fork.

To prepare the dressing, combine the lemon juice, olive oil, salt, and black pepper in a large bowl.

Add the roasted vegetables and cooked quinoa to the dressing and mix thoroughly.

Right before serving, fold in the green onions, pine nuts, and basil. Season to taste.

Sprinkle the feta on top and serve warm or at room temperature.

To take to lunch, pack a serving of the quinoa salad (and pack the feta separately). When you get to school, sprinkle on the feta and dig in!

CREAMY POTATO LEEK SOUP

My family has been making this soup for years. I remember being a little kid and absolutely loving this soup because of how velvety and smooth it is. I would often pick the leeks we grow in our garden to use in this soup. Leeks add the sweet, deep flavor that makes this super yummy. This soup is also creamy, but it has no cream or milk, which is a total bonus.

YIELDS: **4 to 6 servings**
TIME: **45 minutes**

INGREDIENTS:

½ cup/1 stick/113 g unsalted butter (or a dairy-free butter alternative)

2 leeks, sliced thinly and cleaned thoroughly

1 teaspoon salt

½ teaspoon freshly ground black pepper

1 tablespoon tapioca starch or cornstarch

4 cups/946 ml chicken stock

2 large Yukon gold potatoes, peeled and diced (about 4 cups/440 g)

Salt and freshly ground black pepper

74

thermos soups

There is nothing as comforting as steaming hot soup. If you use a thermos, no matter what type of soup you have, it will stay nice and warm until you get the chance to eat it. All you have to do is heat them up, pop them in a thermos, and you're good to go! If there are noodles or croutons in the soup, just pack those on the side and add them once you get to school so they don't get soggy.

DIRECTIONS:

Melt the butter in a large pot over medium heat. Cook the leeks in butter with salt and pepper, stirring frequently, until tender, about 15 minutes. In a bowl, whisk the starch into 1 cup of the chicken broth until it has dissolved, making sure there are no lumps. Pour the starch mixture and remaining stock into the pot.

Add the potatoes and bring to a boil. Lower the heat to low and simmer, partially covered, for about 20 minutes, or until the potatoes are fork-tender.

Working in batches, place about ⅓ of the soup in a blender. Put the lid on but remove the cap, and cover the hole with a kitchen towel. Blend until creamy and smooth. Repeat for the rest of the soup.

Add more salt and pepper to taste, and serve.

CHICKEN SAUSAGE AND KALE SOUP

Every year, my giant extended family has a soup bar on Christmas Eve, where everyone brings a soup or side dish. The kitchen counter is lined with slow cookers steaming with hot soup! This Chicken Sausage and Kale Soup is always a hit. By the end of the night, the pot is scraped clean and everyone is happy and full. I use chicken sausage and a little bit of nitrate-free bacon to give this soup lots of extra flavor. It's so delicious and the all the amazing flavor soaks into the kale. Bonus: kale adds vitamins and fiber too, helping to fight disease! This soup is truly *amazing*!

YIELDS: **6 servings**
TIME: **25 minutes**

INGREDIENTS:

4 slices bacon, cut into ½-inch/ 1.5 cm pieces

1 pound/455 g mild Italian chicken sausage

1 large yellow onion, diced

1 tablespoon peeled and pressed garlic

3 cups/200 g fresh kale

4 cups/905 ml chicken stock

Salt and freshly ground black pepper

DIRECTIONS:

In a large pot or Dutch oven, cook the bacon over medium-high heat until crisp. Scoop out the bacon and set aside on a plate lined with a paper towel. Add the sausage to the bacon drippings in the pot and cook through until crumbly. Remove the sausage and add it to the plate with the bacon.

Leave a few tablespoons of drippings in the bottom of the pot. Add the onion and garlic and cook until the onion is translucent.

Wash and stem the kale. You can do this by holding the stem with one hand and running the other hand down the stem from base to tip, ripping off the leaves in the process. Tear into bite-size pieces.

Add the chicken stock, as well as the bacon and sausage, to the pot and bring to a simmer. Add the kale just before serving and mix until it wilts. Season with salt and pepper, and enjoy.

mason jar salads

My favorite way to pack a salad for school lunches is to layer it in a mason jar! It's super cute, displays all your salad ingredients, and all you have to do once you get to school is shake it up and eat right out of the jar. It's so easy!

How to make the
perfect mason jar salad:

· Make sure you have a wide-mouth mason jar or tall container, so that you can eat easily right out of the jar.

· Put your dressing at the bottom of the jar.

· For the next layer, add harder veggies or meats that won't soak up the dressing or get soggy.

· Put your lettuce and leafy greens on the top. They are the most likely to get soggy next to the dressing.

· If you have meats or fish in this salad, store the jar in your fridge over-night and pack it in your lunch box with some ice packs so it doesn't spoil.

· Leave some room at the top of the mason jar so there is space to mix the salad.

· All of your friends will be so impressed because this salad is gorgeous and unique!

BASIL GODDESS DRESSING ON TOMATOES AND ROMAINE

No wonder my family calls this our Basil Goddess Dressing . . . it's heavenly! The dressing is creamy, fragrant, tangy, and good on almost anything. I love this dressing drizzled on fresh crisp lettuce and juicy tomatoes from our garden. Sometimes the simplest salads are the best.

YIELDS: **2 cups/475 ml dressing, enough for at least 3 to 4 salads**
TIME: **10 minutes**

INGREDIENTS:

2 garlic cloves, peeled

3 anchovy fillets

1 cup/40 g fresh basil

1 cup/225 g mayonnaise

1 cup/100 g chopped green onions

¼ cup/60 ml freshly squeezed lemon juice

Salt and freshly ground black pepper

2 heads romaine lettuce, chopped

1 pint tomatoes, halved

½ cup/55 g cucumber that has been cut into small bite-size pieces

Fresh chives, chopped, for garnish

DIRECTIONS:

In a food processor, combine the garlic, anchovies, basil, mayonnaise, green onions, lemon juice, and salt and pepper to taste. Process until smooth, scraping the sides a few times in between. Store in the refrigerator until use. It will keep for about 3 days.

Arrange the lettuce, tomatoes, and cucumber on a plate, and drizzle with the dressing.

Sprinkle chopped chives on top for garnish.

TIP

packing lunches

Preparing school lunches can be a huge pain in the butt, so here are some tips to keep things easy, convenient, and fresh:

MAKE YOUR LUNCH AHEAD OF TIME. Taking a few minutes the night before to make your lunch will pay off big time the next morning when you're still half asleep. All you have to do is store your lunch in the fridge and just grab and go!

ADD ICE PACKS. Nobody wants to get sick from spoiled food. To prevent a disaster, just pop a few ice packs in your lunch bag. This will keep everything fresh for when lunch rolls around.

USE A THERMOS. We all love our meals nice and hot, and thermoses are a total lifesaver. My family loves them so much that we have an entire pantry shelf dedicated to our thermos collection.

EMBRACE LEFTOVERS. Most days, my sister and I bring last night's dinner for lunch. If you don't want to eat the same thing as the night before, but you still want to use up your leftovers, check out the "Double-Duty Dinners" section of this book. No waste, no fuss.

party at my place

School's Out!

Whether you are hosting a barbecue (page 91), holiday party (page 99 and 111), or just a fun summer bash (page 81), I've got recipes here that will have your guests coming back for more!

SUMMER BASH

Summer is a great time to get together with your friends and family and throw a party or sleepover. I love it when everyone is outside enjoying the sunny weather, and there is a table covered in amazing food, flowers and decorations are scattered around, and there is upbeat music and laughter in the air. One of the keys to a party like this is simple, light food that is easy to prepare and that everyone will enjoy. What follows are some of my favorite summer dishes.

SALT-GRILLED SHRIMP WITH LEMON BASIL DIPPING SAUCE

Bart van Olphen, one of my friends from Jamie Oliver's Food Tube, shared this traditional cooking method he learned in Madrid and I absolutely love it. The salt distributes heat evenly and crisps the shell. All of the juices and flavors stay in the shrimp, so it's tender and perfectly cooked. It also goes well with my Lemon Basil Dipping Sauce. I use this sauce dip for veggies and meats, but the combo of the shrimp and sauce is my absolute favorite! You can make the dip ahead of time and salt-grill the shrimp once your guests arrive. They will be so impressed!

YIELDS: **4 appetizer servings**
TIME: **30 minutes**

salt-grilled shrimp

INGREDIENTS:

Salt

1 pound/455 g large unpeeled shrimp or prawns

DIRECTIONS:

Heat a *plancha*, cast-iron grill, or skillet over high heat.

Pour lots of salt onto the *plancha*/grill/skillet. You want to create about a ½-inch/1.5 cm- thick "bed" for your shrimp.

Continue to heat the salt. Listen closely: if you hear mild popping sounds from the salt, you know it's hot enough.

Place the shrimp on the salt, making sure not to crowd them. Gently press them into the salt with your fingers or tongs.

Cook for 3 to 4 minutes, or until the bottom half of the shrimp turns color, indicating the bottom half is cooked (time depends on the size of your shrimp).

Flip over, and cook the other side for 3 to 4 minutes more.

Flake any dark salt crusts off the shrimp and transfer to a plate. Let everything cool slightly.

Serve with the Lemon Basil Dipping Sauce (recipe follows), and let guests peel the shrimp themselves.

lemon basil dipping sauce

INGREDIENTS:

1 cup/225 g mayonnaise

¼ to ½ cup/10 to 20 g fresh
basil leaves, chopped

Zest and juice of 1 lemon

2 anchovy fillets

¼ teaspoon freshly ground
black pepper

DIRECTIONS:

Combine the mayonnaise, basil, lemon zest and juice, anchovies, and pepper in a food processor and process until smooth. Scrape down the sides and process one last time.

Cover and refrigerate for at least 1 hour before serving.

POTATO SALAD WITH DIJON-TARRAGON DRESSING

This potato salad is so simple but it's *packed* with flavor. My dressing is tangy, filled with herbs, and has a nice kick to it—and the potatoes soak up all the flavor! Unlike traditional American potato salad, this one uses no mayo, so you don't have to worry about it spoiling during the party.

YIELDS: **8 servings**
TIME: **30 minutes**

INGREDIENTS:

2½ pounds/1.1 kg fingerling potatoes, halved

1 tablespoon kosher salt

2 tablespoons freshly squeezed lemon juice

2 garlic cloves, peeled and pressed

⅔ cup/160 ml extra-virgin olive oil

2 teaspoons Dijon mustard

2 tablespoons Champagne vinegar or white wine vinegar

2 tablespoons minced shallot

3 tablespoons chopped fresh flat-leaf parsley

2 tablespoons chopped fresh tarragon

Salt and freshly ground black pepper

DIRECTIONS:

Place the potatoes in a large pot. Cover with cold water by 1 inch/2.5 cm and season generously with the kosher salt. Bring to a boil. Lower the heat to a simmer and cook until the potatoes are tender and you can easily stick a fork through them, about 15 minutes.

Strain the potatoes and run under cold water to cool slightly.

Meanwhile, in a large bowl, whisk together lemon juice, pressed garlic, oil, mustard, vinegar, shallot, parsley, and tarragon. Season with salt and pepper. Add the potatoes and toss to combine.

Store in the fridge, and serve cold or at room temperature.

FIZZY FRUIT

This is gonna blow your mind! Imagine the fruit's juices replaced with soda . . . yeah, that's what it's like! This method is so much fun and you can carbonate all kinds of fruit. And at the end of the day, it's still a piece of fruit, so it's a healthy snack. I made this for a party and all of my friends were so shocked and impressed. Let's just say, there were no leftovers.

YOU WILL NEED:

A cooler

Dry ice (about 1 pound/455 of dry ice for a 50-quart/47 L cooler)

A few clean towels

INGREDIENTS:

Juicy fruits, such as grapes, strawberries, blueberries, watermelon, satsuma oranges, etc.

DIRECTIONS:

Place a clean towel at the bottom of a cooler chest and, using an oven mitt, place dry ice in your cooler. Cover with another clean towel. Be very careful with the dry ice. The extreme cold can burn you just like extreme heat. Always handle the ice chunks with either a towel or oven mitt to make sure they never have direct contact with your skin.

Wash and dry the fruit, then place it in the prepared cooler, making sure that the fruits are not directly touching the dry ice. You can create a barrier with the towel. If your fruit has thick skin, such as a watermelon, make sure you cut it up into pieces so the gases can reach the juice in the fruit.

Place the lid securely on the cooler and wrap tightly in plastic wrap so it is airtight and no gases can escape. Wrap multiple layers of plastic wrap around the cooler—it takes a lot!

Let sit for 12 to 18 hours. The plastic wrap will most likely be bulging from containing the gases. Unwrap the cooler, serve immediately, and watch your guests be amazed!

GUILT-FREE FUDGE POPS

Who doesn't love fudge pops? Unfortunately, typical fudge pops you buy at the store often have artificial sweeteners, colors, flavors, and preservatives. But if you make your own at home, you can use real foods and natural sweeteners. There is also a secret ingredient inside my version that makes these fudge pops extra creamy, but you will never guess what it is!

YIELDS: **6 pops**
TIME: **5 minutes + 6 hours freezing time**

INGREDIENTS:

2 ripe avocados, peeled and pitted

½ cup/55 g raw cacao powder

½ cup/120 ml pure maple syrup

2 teaspoons pure vanilla extract

1½ cups/355 ml unsweetened almond milk, plus more as needed

Pinch of sea salt

DIRECTIONS:

Combine all the ingredients in a blender and blend until everything is smooth and creamy.

Add more cacao, maple syrup, or salt to taste, and add more almond milk as needed—you want the mixture to be very thick but still pourable.

Pour into your ice pop mold, and let freeze for about 6 hours, or until fully frozen (follow the directions for your particular mold). You may have to run the mold under some water to loosen the pops from the mold.

cacao powder

To all my fellow chocoholics out there, you are going to love what I'm about to tell you: Chocolate can be good for you! Well, at least chocolate that is higher in cacao can be. Cacao powder is what gives chocolate its chocolaty flavor and it's a superfood, filled with tons of nutrients that keep your brain functioning and your skin healthy, and it is even said to be a natural mood elevator. It's the ultimate teen weapon!

BACKYARD CAMPOUT

I love roasting things over the fire, getting food all caramelized and relishing that extra-smoky flavor. My family
has a fire pit in our backyard, and we love inviting friends
and family over to enjoy it with us. Whether making sweet
treats or savory dinners, everyone's going to have a blast
creating these dishes and hanging out by the campfire.

TOMATO AND
BASIL BRUSCHETTA

My mom once took a cooking class in Italy and one of the most important things she learned was that you only need a few good, quality ingredients to make a fantastic dish. Bruschetta is a perfect example. The tomatoes are sweet, the basil fragrant, and the garlic gives it a savory kick. Then, you pile all of it onto a small piece of crunchy, buttery, golden brown crostini and you get an explosion of flavors. Less is more definitely applies to this recipe.

YIELDS: **4 servings**

TIME: **10 minutes**

INGREDIENTS:

Bruschetta:

2 large ripe tomatoes

1 garlic clove, peeled and pressed

¼ cup/10 g basil, cut into ribbons

2 tablespoons olive oil

Salt and pepper

Crostini:

½ small baguette

1 garlic clove

DIRECTIONS:

Chop the tomatoes. Place them in a bowl along with the garlic and basil. Add enough olive oil to lightly coat and add salt and pepper to taste. Mix well.

To make the crostini, slice half a small baguette. Toast the slices of baguette, then lightly rub one side with the garlic clove. Top with the bruschetta and serve.

HOT DOG OCTOPUS

The perfect backyard campout wouldn't be complete without a campfire and some hot dogs. But don't settle for regular ol' hot dogs; skip the bun and watch this golden, crispy, smoky octopus come to life in front of your eyes! Make sure to buy nitrate-free, organic hot dogs, and you've upgraded the plain hot dog to a party-worthy dish.

YIELDS: **1 serving**
TIME: **5 minutes**

INGREDIENTS:

1 nitrate-free hot dog

DIRECTIONS:

Using a knife, slice the bottom half of the hot dog lengthwise. Keep cutting until you have 8 "legs."

Poke a store-bought hot dog roasting stick horizontally through the "head" of the octopus so the octopus is standing upright when placed over the campfire.

Keep the octopus upright. The legs will start to curl upward away from the flames as they cook. Once the legs are cooked enough that they are fairly firm and not flimsy, you can turn the octopus upside down to cook its head.

Carefully remove your octopus from the hot dog stick, and serve with your favorite condiments.

GREEN BEAN SALAD WITH TANGY MUSTARD VINAIGRETTE

This salad is one of my all-time favorite veggie dishes. The green beans still have a crunch to them, there is a bit of bite from the red onion, and the nutty almonds and a creamy tangy dressing all come together into a perfect summer side dish.

YIELDS: **4 to 6 servings**
TIME: **15 minutes**

INGREDIENTS:

1 pound/455 g green beans

¼ cup/28 g slivered almonds

2 tablespoons extra-virgin olive oil

1 tablespoon red wine vinegar

1 tablespoon Dijon mustard

Salt and freshly ground black pepper

1 shallot, minced (about 2 tablespoons)

¼ cup/15 g finely chopped fresh parsley leaves

DIRECTIONS:

Wash and trim off the ends of the green beans. Cut them in half or into bite-size pieces.

Using a steamer of your choice, steam the beans for about 4 minutes, or until they turn bright green and are just cooked but still crunchy and not mushy. Strain the beans and shock them in ice water to stop the cooking.

Toast the slivered almonds in a dry skillet over medium-low heat until golden brown and fragrant. Be careful not to burn them! It should only take a few minutes.

In a large bowl, whisk together the olive oil, vinegar, and mustard until creamy. Season to taste with salt and pepper.

To the bowl, add the green beans, shallot, parsley, and almonds. Mix until everything is coated with the dressing.

Serve warm, cold, or at room temperature.

GRANDMA'S CHICKEN APPLE SALAD

I live in the state of Washington, where the state fruit is the apple! I love using tart and sweet Granny Smith apples for my grandma's chicken apple salad, which is sweet, savory, tart, and creamy. The awesome thing about this recipe is that you can make it the day before so the flavors have time to meld together. Then, all you have to do is pull it out of the fridge right before your party!

YIELDS: **8 servings**
TIME: **20 minutes**

INGREDIENTS:

Salad:

2 large green apples (such as Granny Smith), chopped into bite-size pieces

4 large celery stalks, chopped

4 cooked chicken breasts, cooled and shredded

4 green onions, sliced thinly

Dressing:

2 large eggs

½ teaspoon salt

¼ teaspoon garlic powder

½ teaspoon dry mustard

¼ teaspoon freshly ground black pepper

¼ cup/60 ml apple cider vinegar

1 cup/235 ml extra-virgin olive oil

DIRECTIONS:

Combine the salad ingredients in a big bowl.

Prepare the dressing: Place the eggs, salt, garlic powder, dry mustard, pepper, and vinegar in a food processor. Pulse until everything is combined. While the food processor is running, slowly drizzle in the olive oil for a thick, creamy dressing. Warning: The dressing by itself doesn't taste great; actually, it's a little bitter. But once it's had time to sit with the apples, celery, chicken, and green onions, it becomes amazing!

Pour the dressing over the salad and toss to coat evenly.

Refrigerate overnight. The next day, adjust the seasonings if necessary, toss, and serve.

CAMPFIRE MOCHI
SANDWICHES

Are you looking for an alternative to s'mores? Here's something that I think is even better than s'mores, and it also happens to be dairy-free, gluten-free, and corn-free! The awesome thing about this dessert is that you can stuff them with anything you want—personally, I love dark chocolate and peanut butter with jam. This is my favorite campfire treat!

Mochi, originally from Japan, is sweet rice that has been pounded and dried into shapes. You can get *mochi* at any Asian grocery store or possibly in the international section in your local store. Sometimes it is in the refrigerated section, so check there if you don't see it in the aisles.

YIELDS: **1 serving**
TIME: **5 minutes**

INGREDIENTS:

Nonstick cooking spray

Dried *mochi*, cut into squares (I cut mine into 2-inch/5 cm squares; some come already cut)

Your favorite stuffing, such as nut butter, jelly, and high-quality dark chocolate

DIRECTIONS:

Spray the inside of your grill basket or grate placed over the campfire with nonstick cooking spray. Place several *mochi* in the basket or on the grate.

Roast the *mochi*, taking care not to burn it, until it's crispy on the outside and gooey on the inside. Be patient! It should take 5 to 7 minutes.

Carefully cut a slit in the side of the *mochi*, creating a pocket, and stuff with your favorite toppings.

Let the stuffing heat up and melt (a minute or so). This also allows the *mochi* to cool a bit so you can pick it up to eat it.

HALLOWEEN PARTY

Most of us think of candy when we think of Halloween, and it's usually followed by a sugar hangover the next day. Battle the sugar binge by inviting your friends over before you go out trick-or-treating to munch on these awesome, creepy, and fun Halloween dishes. They are sure to balance out the candy bars in your trick-or-treat bag. Who says Halloween has to be all about the sugar?

PUKING PEPPERS

Ewwwwww! These Puking Peppers are the perfect thing to eat before going trick-or-treating. They are a blast to make, and by mixing regular pasta and zucchini noodles, you can make this recipe even healthier. This is a super spooky way to serve your noodles.

YIELDS: **1 serving**
TIME: **15 minutes**

INGREDIENTS:

1 bell pepper

½ cup/60 g zucchini noodles, made with a vegetable spiralizer or sliced thinly with a mandoline and cut into thin strips with a knife

½ cup/70 g cooked spaghetti

¼ cup/63 g pasta sauce (choose your favorite!)

DIRECTIONS:

Cut off the top of the pepper and remove the seeds and white flesh.

Using a pumpkin carving tool or a small paring knife, carve a big mouth and eyes from the front of the pepper.

In a bowl, combine the zucchini noodles, cooked spaghetti, and sauce.

Using clean hands or tongs, stuff your pepper with the noodle mixture and pull some strands out of the mouth of the pepper.

Place the top of the pepper back on (or leave it off to have the brains "spill out") and serve. Have fun with it!

GNARLY CARROT FINGERS IN BLACK BEAN DIP

These are *so creepy* and super fun to put together! This dip is simple and packed with flavor. It's creamy, tangy, and a little spicy, and goes well with veggies and chips. Everyone is going to be so impressed by the presentation of your dish!

YIELDS: **About 4 cups/1 kg, 10 to 12 servings (for full recipe with 2 cans of beans)**

TIME: **10 minutes**

INGREDIENTS:

½ cup/80 g chopped yellow onion

⅓ cup/13 g fresh cilantro

1 garlic clove, peeled

1 to 2 tablespoons minced jalapeño pepper

¼ cup/60 ml freshly squeezed lime juice

¼ teaspoon ground cumin

1 teaspoon salt

½ teaspoon freshly ground black pepper

1 teaspoon hot sauce

2 (15-ounce/425 g) cans black beans, drained and rinsed

TO ASSEMBLE:

5 crooked carrots

½ onion, peeled

5 sliced or silvered almonds

DIRECTIONS:

In a food processor, pulse the chopped onion, cilantro, garlic, and jalapeño until everything is minced.

Add the lime juice, cumin, salt, black pepper, hot sauce, and black beans and pulse until smooth. Add up to 2 tablespoons of water if the dip is too thick.

To assemble: Line up the carrots and decide which is going to be the thumb, pinkie finger, and so on. Vary the heights accordingly.

Cut the bottom of the carrots so that when they are standing up, they are at the right height.

Put the black bean dip in a bowl. The onion will serve as a base for holding the carrot fingers. Place the ½ onion, flat-side down, on a cutting board. Pierce a toothpick halfway into the bottom of each carrot, and pierce the other half of the toothpick into the onion. Repeat with all carrot fingers and the carrot thumb, arranging them so that they look like a hand reaching upward. If it doesn't look right the first time, no problem! Just pull the carrots and toothpicks out of the onion and try again. Carefully place carrot-studded onion into the dip. If necessary, spoon the dip around the base of the carrots to hide the onion.

To create the fingernails, use a little bit of bean dip to glue an almond to the tip of each carrot.

CREEPY APPLE BITES

Halloween can be fun *and* healthy. These creepy apple bites are spooky and so delicious! My sister and I made these every year as little kids. They are fun to assemble and they look amazing . . . but as soon as they were made, they were devoured.

YIELDS: **4 big "bites" per apple**
TIME: **10 minutes**

INGREDIENTS:

½ large apple, cut into 8 wedges

¼ cup/65 g creamy peanut butter

2 all-natural fruit roll-ups

Small handful of slivered almonds

DIRECTIONS:

Spread 1½ teaspoons of peanut butter on one side of each apple slice.

Cut about a 2½-inch/6.5 cm strip of the fruit roll-up, and then cut one end round so it's shaped like a tongue. Drape it over one apple slice.

Stab slivered almonds into the outer edge of the apple to create teeth.

Place the apple slice without the fruit roll-up over the other to complete this tasty, spooky snack.

CHERRY LIME PUNCH WITH FROZEN HAND

Creep out your friends with this scary cherry limeade, complete with a floating ice hand (that helps your drink stay cold). This is probably the coolest-looking drink I have ever made in my life. It's creepy-awesome!!!

YIELDS: **8 servings**

TIME: **10 minutes plus freezing time for hand and chilling time for bowl**

INGREDIENTS:

Frozen hand equipment:

Tight fitting gloves such as vinyl gloves (avoid latex gloves, as some people are allergic to them)

Drinking water

Rubber bands

Punch bowl décor:

3 tablespoons golden syrup or light corn syrup

Red food coloring

Small plastic spiders

For each quart/946 ml of cherry limeade (how much depends on the size of your bowl):

½ cup/120 ml freshly squeezed lime juice

1 cup/235 ml unsweetened cherry juice

4 to 5 cups/946 ml to 1.2 L chilled sparkling water

1½ to 2 teaspoons liquid stevia, or to taste

DIRECTIONS:

If possible, chill your punch bowl and all ingredients ahead of time. That way, your hand ice cube will last longer.

The night before (or earlier), make your ice hand by filling a vinyl glove with drinking water (avoid latex gloves, since some people are allergic to them), tying it off with a rubber band, and placing it in the freezer. For best results, let it rest over an upside-down bowl so it is a bit cupped— it will look more natural that way.

To decorate your punch bowl, take some golden syrup and mix it with red food coloring until you get the bloody color you want. Make sure your bowl is placed on a surface that doesn't stain.

Carefully drip the red syrup around the edge of your bowl, letting some drip down the outer edge.

Place some plastic spiders on the syrup—it's perfect glue!

Refrigerate the bowl until ready to use and also to harden the syrup a bit.

Before your party, combine all the limeade ingredients in the bowl.

Retrieve your ice hand from the freezer, use a paring knife to cut the glove open, and carefully peel it off the ice.

Gently place the ice hand in the limeade and serve. I recommend making a few ice hands, so that you have extras in case one breaks, and also so you can replace them as they start to melt in the punch. That way you can keep the creepy factor going throughout the whole party.

JACK-O'-LANTERN BABIES

These are one of the easiest Halloween-themed snacks to make! Take some clementines and draw scary faces on them with a black permanent marker, and *BAM*! You have mini Jack-O'-Lanterns! These can be used as decoration as well as a snack. When you peel the clementines, the marker is removed, so you don't have to worry about eating ink.

TIP

what to do about
all that candy?

Here's the scene at our house after trick-or-treating: My sister and our friends dump our loot onto the floor and organize the candy by type and color. Then, we trade. Sound familiar? But here's the part that's maybe a bit different from what you might do. Instead of binge-ing on the candy, we pick a few that we love and donate the rest to soldiers serving overseas. The soldiers get a little something sweet from home and we still get some candy, but we also avoid the sugar hangover the next day. There are several charities offering this service, so research online to find the one you like.

SPRINGSGIVING

I absolutely *love* Thanksgiving, but around springtime, I start to crave those amazing holiday flavors again. A few years ago, my family decided that we wanted to celebrate Thanksgiving twice a year . . . and so Springsgiving was born! The rules of Springsgiving are simple: stressing is not allowed, and everyone has to show up to the dinner table in their pajamas (my sister always shows up in a onesie, and I always have on my fuzzy socks). Springsgiving is a great way to spend awesome time with friends and family and to indulge in ultimate comfort foods . . . without waiting until next November.

HERB, NUT, AND CRANBERRY SPREAD

I love plating dishes, so putting this beautiful dish together is so much fun! This creamy, savory spread is made with vegetables, herbs, and seeds that have been baked golden, then mixed with sweet dried cranberries before being covered with crunchy almonds. Spread it on a buttery cracker for a taste and texture explosion!

YIELDS: **3 pinecones, 10 to 12 servings**
TIME: **1 hour 40 minutes (20 minutes prep, 1 hour cooking, 20 minutes assembly)**

INGREDIENTS:

1 potato

1 large carrot

1 yellow onion

1 celery stalk

1 garlic clove, peeled and pressed

1 teaspoon dried thyme

½ teaspoon dried basil leaves

½ teaspoon dried sage

½ teaspoon dried savory

½ teaspoon dry mustard

1 cup/145 g sunflower seeds

½ cup/65 g whole wheat flour

½ cup/64 g nutritional yeast

¾ teaspoon salt

½ teaspoon freshly ground black pepper

½ cup/120 ml vegetable oil, plus more for baking dish

2 tablespoons freshly squeezed lemon juice

¾ cup/90 g dried cranberries, chopped

TO ASSEMBLE AND SERVE:

2 to 3 cups/290 to 435 g almonds

Rosemary sprigs

Crackers for serving (we use buttery round crackers)

DIRECTIONS:

Peel and chop the potato, carrot, onion, and celery into large chunks.

Place the chopped veggies, garlic, 1½ cups/355 ml of water, and the remaining ingredients, except the cranberries, in a food processor. Process until smooth. Make sure to scrape down the sides.

Pour the mixture into an oiled 11 x 9-inch/29 x 23 cm baking dish, and make sure it's in an even layer. Bake at 350°F/180°C for an hour, or until the mixture is fluffy and the liquid is absorbed.

Spoon the spread into a large bowl and add the chopped cranberries. Mix well and then cool for 30 minutes or more in the refrigerator.

This mixture will make three small or two large pinecones. Take a big handful of the mixture and shape it into a pinecone, with one pointed end and one rounded end. Place it on a plate, making sure to leave room for the rosemary sprigs. Repeat for your other pinecones.

Starting at the tip of your pinecone and working your way from the tip to the back, place the almonds close together on the mixture, with the pointed end of each almond facing the pointed end of the pinecone.

Place the rosemary sprigs around the pinecones, and serve with crackers.

ROAST TURKEY BREAST WITH GRAVY

The turkey is the star of the show on any Thanksgiving or Springsgiving table, but cooking a whole turkey can be a lot of work. No worries, I've got you covered. If you want to save time but still want turkey on your special day, here is a super easy recipe to get golden brown, moist, flavorful turkey breast and savory pan gravy that the whole family will love!

YIELDS: **6 to 8 servings**
TIME: **3 hours (30 minutes prep, 2½ hours roasting)**

INGREDIENTS:

1 (6-pound/2.7 kg) fresh bone-in turkey breast, rinsed and patted dry

2 tablespoons unsalted butter, melted (or a dairy-free butter alternative)

1 tablespoon salt

¾ teaspoon freshly ground black pepper

Zest of ½ lemon (reserve the zested lemon)

1 celery stalk

1 medium-size carrot

1 medium-size onion

Leaves from 2 thyme sprigs

¼ cup/30 g all-purpose flour

2 cups/475 ml chicken or turkey stock

DIRECTIONS:

Pat the turkey dry with paper towels. Brush melted butter all over the turkey breast, including inside the cavity, then sprinkle salt, pepper, and lemon zest on top.

Chop the celery, carrot, and onion into 1- to 2-inch/2.5 to 5 cm chunks. Cut the zested lemon into quarters and toss them in a bowl with the thyme and chopped vegetables.

Place the ⅔ of the vegetable mixture in the bottom of a roasting pan. Add ¼ cup/60 ml of water to the bottom of the pan. Place the turkey, breast-side up, in the pan, on top of the vegetables. Place the remaining ⅓ of the vegetable mixture inside the turkey cavity.

Roast the turkey in a 325°F/170°F oven for 2 to 2½ hours, or until an instant-read meat thermometer reads 165°F/74°C in the thickest part of the breast.

Tent the turkey with foil and let it rest for 20 to 30 minutes before carving.

While the turkey is resting, pour the drippings into a separate cup or fat-separator cup to remove all but 3 tablespoons of fat from the drippings. Pour the reserved fat and juices back into the roasting pan. Bring the heat to medium high, and use a wooden spoon to scrape off browned bits from the bottom of the pan.

Stir in the flour and cook, stirring constantly, for 2 minutes. Whisk in the stock, making sure to whisk away any clumps. Bring to a simmer and cook until it reaches your desired thickness, about 3 minutes. Put the gravy through a strainer and discard the vegetables. Season with salt and pepper to taste.

Carve the turkey and serve with gravy. FYI: These leftovers are great for lunch!

CINNAMON THYME SWEET POTATO PUREE

Back in 2016, I visited my friend Gibson Borelli (winner of *Rachael vs. Guy*, season 2) and we cooked dinner together. We decided to randomly create our own sweet potato purée going by nothing but our taste buds. Both of us fell in love with our creation and I took the recipe home to Seattle. Since then, I've tweaked it a bit, including swapping coconut milk for the heavy cream, and now it's a total staple on our Thanksgiving/Springsgiving table! It's creamy, velvety, and the cinnamon and thyme really bring out the holiday flavors. Thank you, Gibson!

YIELDS: **6 to 8 servings**
TIME: **30 minutes**

INGREDIENTS:

¼ cup/½ stick/55 g unsalted butter (or a dairy-free butter alternative)

4 cups/440 g peeled and cubed sweet potato (1-inch/2.5 cm cubes)

1 cup/140 g peeled, seeded, and cubed butternut squash (1-inch/2.5 cm cubes)

1 teaspoon ground cinnamon

½ teaspoon chopped fresh thyme

½ cup/120 ml (or more) chicken or vegetable stock, or water

¼ to ½ cup/60 to 120 ml canned coconut milk cream (the thick coconut cream that you find at the top of a can of coconut milk)

Salt and freshly ground black pepper

sweet potato

I love sweet potatoes! They are sweet, creamy, and overall heavenly. But did you know that sweet potatoes are actually much healthier than regular potatoes? They are loaded with vitamin A, which is key to having good vision. That's super important for school so that you can see the board and all that . . . fun stuff.

DIRECTIONS:

Over medium heat, melt the butter in a big pot and add the sweet potato, squash, cinnamon, thyme, and stock. Partially cover and let simmer over medium-low heat for about 20 minutes, until the vegetables are completely soft. Stir occasionally, and add more stock if it gets too dry.

When the vegetables are soft, transfer into a food processor and pulse a few times to break up the mixture. Then, while the food processor is running, drop in spoonfuls of the coconut cream until the mixture has reached the desired thickness and it is velvety smooth.

Taste and season with salt and pepper. Pulse the food processor a few times to make sure the salt and pepper are incorporated, and serve.

ROASTED CAULIFLOWER WITH GARLIC HERB DRIZZLE

My grandma didn't like cauliflower until she had this recipe—and then she was converted. So, if you think you don't like cauliflower, try this recipe and think again! It's perfectly roasted yet still has a slight bite to it, and I drizzle a fragrant herb oil over it that is to die for. This herb drizzle is great over all different types of grilled veggies, but it tastes the best over cauliflower, in my opinion.

This recipe makes ¼ cup/60 ml of the Garlic Herb Drizzle, but you only need a portion of that for this dish. Save the rest for drizzling over veggies or chicken! It's *that* good!

YIELDS: **6 servings**
TIME: **30 minutes**

INGREDIENTS:

1 head cauliflower

Grapeseed oil

¼ cup/60 ml extra-virgin olive oil

¼ teaspoon dried oregano

¼ teaspoon dried basil

¼ teaspoon dried rosemary

¼ teaspoon kosher salt

Freshly ground black pepper

Pinch of red pepper flakes

3 garlic cloves, peeled and pressed

DIRECTIONS:

Preheat the oven to 450°F/230°F.

Cut the cauliflower into bite-size florets and place on a baking sheet, making sure the cauliflower is not crowded. You may need to use 2 baking sheets.

Drizzle with some grapeseed oil, just enough to lightly coat the cauliflower. Toss with your hands to coat.

Roast in the oven for about 20 minutes, or until the edges are browned and crispy.

While the cauliflower is roasting, place the olive oil, oregano, basil, rosemary, salt, pepper, red pepper flakes, and garlic in a small saucepan and stir. Heat the drizzle just until the garlic starts sizzling, and then remove from the heat.

Place the hot cauliflower on a plate and drizzle with the Garlic Herb Drizzle, making sure to get some of the garlic and herbs onto every bit of cauliflower. Serve immediately.

MUSHROOM AND SAUSAGE STUFFING

Of all the dishes I make for Thanksgiving and Springsgiving, this mushroom stuffing is, hands down, my favorite. I always make a double batch so that I can eat it for days. My dad loves it just as much as I do, and we always fight over the leftovers!

This stuffing has tons of mushrooms and is packed with veggies, sausage, and bread cubes that soak up all the juices and flavor. Because I make it in a slow cooker, it's super moist, and all I have to do is some initial prep, then I can sit back and watch it do its thing! Remember how "no stress" is a Springsgiving requirement? This recipe definitely fits the bill.

YIELDS: **10 to 12 servings**
TIME: **45 minutes prep, 5 hours cooking time**

INGREDIENTS:

¾ cup/1½ sticks/167 g unsalted butter (or a dairy-free butter alternative)

2 cups/320 g chopped onion

2 cups/200 g chopped celery

1 pound/455 g mushrooms, sliced

½ cup/30 g fresh parsley, chopped

1 pound/455 g mild Italian sausage

12 cups/680 g dry bread cubes (I recommend larger cubes from crusty bread, so the stuffing has more texture)

1 tablespoon poultry seasoning

1½ teaspoons salt

½ teaspoon freshly ground black pepper

Up to 4 cups/946 ml chicken stock, as needed

2 large eggs, beaten

Nonstick cooking spray

DIRECTIONS:

Melt the butter in a big skillet over medium heat. Cook the onion, celery, mushrooms, and parsley in the butter, stirring frequently.

Once the veggies are cooked, 5 to 7 minutes, remove from the heat and transfer them to a bowl. Add the sausage to the empty pan and cook until fully cooked and crumbly.

Place the bread cubes in a very large mixing bowl and spoon the cooked vegetables and cooked sausage over the bread cubes. Season with the poultry seasoning, salt, and pepper. Pour in enough stock to moisten, starting with 2½ cups/590 ml and adding more as needed. Add the eggs and make sure everything is well mixed.

Spray the inside of a slow cooker with nonstick cooking spray. Transfer the mixture to the slow cooker and cover.

Cook on HIGH for 45 minutes. Then, lower the heat to LOW and cook for 8 hours, or cook for 4 hours on HIGH.

Check the stuffing periodically, and add more stock if the bread cubes are getting dry.

SIMPLY ROASTED
BRUSSELS SPROUTS

I used to hate Brussels sprouts until I had them roasted like this. Now, I will eat these little guys like candy! They're smoky and tender, with crispy, caramelized edges. This is a perfect veggie side dish at any Thanksgiving/Springsgiving table.

YIELDS: **4 servings**
TIME: **25 minutes**

INGREDIENTS:

1 pound/455 g Brussels sprouts, washed

1 tablespoon grapeseed oil

Salt and freshly ground black pepper

DIRECTIONS:

Preheat the oven to 400°F/200°C.

Cut off the bottom of the Brussels sprouts and peel off any wilted or browned outer leaves. If any sprouts are very large, cut them in half lengthwise so they are all about the same size.

Toss the sprouts in just enough oil to coat. Sprinkle with salt and pepper.

Put them on a baking sheet and roast for 20 to 30 minutes, or until crispy on the outside and cooked through, shaking the baking sheet occasionally to make sure they aren't sticking. Serve immediately.

CRANBERRY SAUCE, 3 WAYS

My sister is in charge of making cranberry sauce every year because it is one of her favorite things about Thanksgiving/Springsgiving. She makes not one, not two, but *three* deliciously different cranberry sauces: classic sauce, maple-cinnamon sauce, and orange-cranberry sauce. They are all so good I can't choose a favorite!

YIELDS: **About 2 cups/500 g per sauce**
TIME: **10 minutes each**

classic cranberry sauce

INGREDIENTS:

¾ cup/150 g sugar

¾ cup/175 ml water

¼ teaspoon salt

12 ounces/340 g fresh cranberries, washed and picked through

maple-cinnamon cranberry sauce

INGREDIENTS:

¾ cup/175 ml pure maple syrup

¼ cup/60 ml water

¼ teaspoon salt

1 cinnamon stick

12 ounces/340 g fresh cranberries, washed and picked through

orange-cranberry sauce

INGREDIENTS:

½ cup/100 g sugar

¾ cup/175 ml freshly squeezed orange juice

¼ teaspoon salt

12 ounces/340 g fresh cranberries, washed and picked through

DIRECTIONS:

In a nonreactive saucepan over high heat, bring all the ingredients, except the cranberries, to a boil so the salt dissolves.

Add the cranberries and bring back to a boil.

Lower the heat to medium and stir until most of the cranberries have popped and the sauce thickens.

Let cool in a bowl and serve. You can make this up to a week in advance and store it in the fridge.

how to throw a successful party

Throwing a party doesn't have to be a lot of work. The key ingredient is a friend (or ten)! Here are some tips so you can relax knowing that everyone is going to have a total blast:

· Prep ahead. Do as much food prep ahead of time as you can. Think about what you can prechop or cook and store until the party. This will make your life so much easier when it comes time to cook and assemble everything. The less you have to do once your friends arrive, the better!

· Get your friends involved. Have them come over early and help you decorate or cook. You may be surprised by how eager your friends are to help! Plus, it makes the prep (and the party) way more fun.

· Create a party music playlist. Music makes things way more fun and it's an absolute must for a party. A music playlist totally adds to the mood and you can customize your songs according to the party theme.

· Put out easy snacks before guests arrive. Think about having roasted nuts or a salami and cheese plate ready for your guest upon arrival. If dinner isn't ready yet but people are already hungry, then they'll have something to munch on without getting too full.

family meals

Family meals are super important. It's a time when everyone sits down after a long day of work or school and enjoys delicious food together. My family makes a point to have everyone sit down at the table together every night during the week for dinner, and during the weekends we will often invite family or friends to join our meals. The following are some of my and my family's favorite meals to share together.

AWARD-WINNING NO-NOODLE LASAGNA

Former First Lady Michelle Obama hosted the Healthy Lunchtime Challenge in 2013, calling out to kids and parents across the country to submit an original healthy recipe that would inspire families to cook together and eat wholesome meals. I submitted this recipe and won for the state of Washington! I had the honor of dining next to the First Lady and meeting President Obama, and I also chatted with many amazing kids and parents who think that fresh, delicious food is the best kind of food.

This lasagna ditches pasta and uses zucchini as the noodles, and trust me, it tastes *so good*. My family eats the whole pan every time! If the White House kitchen staff and First Lady Michelle Obama approve of this lasagna, I think you will, too.

YIELDS: **6 to 8 servings**
TIME: **1 hour, 15 minutes + drying time for the zucchini**

INGREDIENTS:

3 medium-size zucchini

2 tablespoons grapeseed oil

1 cup/160 g chopped yellow onion
(about 1 onion)

2 garlic cloves, peeled and pressed

1 pound/455 g Italian turkey sausage,
casings removed

1 (28-ounce/800 g) can crushed
tomatoes in tomato purée

1 (6-ounce/170 g) can tomato paste

1 tablespoon dried basil leaves

½ to 1 teaspoon kosher salt

½ teaspoon freshly ground
black pepper

8 ounces/225 g mozzarella cheese,
shredded

2 ounces/55 g Parmesan cheese,
grated

zucchini

Most people know that zucchini is healthy, but I bet you didn't realize it is also a good source of vitamin C. Not only does vitamin C strengthen your immune system, but it also can improve your mood! Another great reason to add zucchini to your shopping list.

DIRECTIONS:

Preheat the oven to 400°F/200°C.

Slice the zucchini lengthwise with a mandoline so that they are paper-thin strips. Set out the strips on paper towels to dry out while you make the sauce.

Heat the oil in a large (10- to 12-inch/25.5 to 30.5 cm) skillet. Add the onion and cook for 5 minutes over medium-low heat, until translucent. Add the garlic and cook for 1 minute more.

Add the sausage and cook over medium heat, breaking it up with a wooden spoon, for 8 to 10 minutes, or until it's no longer pink and crumbly.

Add the tomatoes, tomato paste, basil, ½ to 1 teaspoon salt (depending on taste and the saltiness of your sausage), and the pepper. Simmer, uncovered, over medium-low heat for 15 to 20 minutes, until thickened.

To assemble the lasagna, ladle about ¾ cup/175 ml of the sauce into a 13 x 9 x 2-inch/33 x 23 x 5 cm rectangular baking dish, spreading the sauce over the bottom of the dish. Layer the zucchini, overlapping them slightly. Sprinkle with a small handful of mozzarella, a bit of Parmesan, and then another ladle full of sauce. Repeat until you are out of ingredients, finishing with sauce, topped with Parmesan. Bake for 30 minutes, until the sauce is bubbling. Broil for a minute or two at the end to get a nice crust. Let it cool slightly so that it can set before serving.

MOM'S CREAMY CHICKEN STEW

Cream stew is a comfort food in Japan, and my mom grew up eating it. But it always came from a box and was filled with MSG and chemicals. So, when Lexi and I were little, Mom created a homemade version and it has become a staple in the Kelley house. It is filled with fresh, natural ingredients and reminds me a lot of chicken potpie filling. It makes great leftovers, too, so consider making a double batch!

YIELDS: **about 2 quarts/1.9 L, 6 servings**
TIME: **45 minutes**

INGREDIENTS:

4 cups/946 ml chicken stock, preferably homemade

½ cup/1 stick/113 g unsalted butter (or a dairy-free butter alternative)

1 cup/160 g chopped yellow onion (about 1 onion)

½ cup/60 g all-purpose flour

4 cups/560 g cooked and shredded chicken

1 small potato, cubed (about 1 cup/110 g)

4 medium-size carrots, diced (2 cups/260 g)

1 cup/130 g frozen small whole onions (pearl onions)

Salt and freshly ground black pepper

1 cup/130 g frozen peas

Cooked rice for serving

Fresh parsley for garnish

DIRECTIONS:

Heat the chicken stock in a pot.

In a separate large pot or Dutch oven, melt the butter and sauté the yellow onion over medium-low heat for about 5 minutes, until translucent.

Add the flour and cook over low heat, stirring constantly, for 2 minutes.

Add the hot chicken stock to the pot a bit at time, to prevent clumping. Simmer over low heat for 1 minute, stirring, until thickened.

Add the chicken, potato, carrots, and pearl onions and cook for about 20 minutes, or until the potato and carrot are fork-tender, stirring occasionally.

Add the peas, mix well, and heat through. Add salt and pepper to taste.

Ladle the cream stew over hot rice, sprinkle with parsley, and serve. If you'd like, you can let it cool, refrigerate, and reheat the next day. The flavors will really blend and the stew will become even more delicious.

NANA'S OKONOMIYAKI
(SAVORY JAPANESE PANCAKE)

Okonomiyaki is a savory Japanese pancake topped with meat and a variety of delicious condiments. It's a mix of great flavors and textures that meld together perfectly. It's super popular in Japan, and if you give it a try you will understand why. *Okonomi* translates to "as you like," and different regions of Japan have their own styles of this dish (and every family has its favorite). This is my nana's version—if you ask me, hers is the best!

This recipe calls for grated Japanese yam. It's a small amount, but don't be tempted to leave it out. It makes the pancakes extra fluffy and delicious.

YIELDS: **3 large pancakes, 2 to 3 servings**
TIME: **45 minutes + chilling time for the batter**

INGREDIENTS:

Batter (makes 1 large or 3 small pancakes):

½ cup/120 ml prepared konbu broth, seaweed broth, or dashi (see directions)

½ cup/60 g all-purpose flour

1 tablespoon grated Japanese yam (also called *yamaimo* or *nagaimo*)

2 pinches of baking soda

Pinch of salt

2 cups/140 g very thinly shredded cabbage

1 large egg

Baby dried shrimp (optional)

1 tablespoon or more grapeseed oil for cooking

Toppings:

1 (5.6-ounce/159 g) package precooked yakisoba noodles

¼ pound/115 g thinly sliced pork

Condiments:

Japanese *tonkatsu* sauce

Mayonnaise (in a squeeze bottle)

Aonori (seaweed sprinkles)

Green onion, chopped

Red pickled ginger (optional)

DIRECTIONS:

If your broth or dashi is in powdered form, make the ½ cup/120 ml of broth according to the package instructions.

Combine the broth, flour, yam, baking soda, and salt in a bowl and mix. Let it sit in the fridge for an hour or more.

While the batter is in the fridge, prepare the yakisoba noodles for the yakisoba. Break up the noodles by soaking in hot (not boiling) water for 1 minute, pulling apart with a fork or chopsticks. Drain immediately.

Take the batter out of the fridge and add shredded cabbage, egg, and shrimp, if using, and mix.

Heat a nonstick 12-inch/35.5 cm skillet over medium-high heat and grease with a teaspoon of grapeseed oil. Alternatively, you can use an electric griddle at the dining table, and have your guests make the pancakes as they eat. Place about ⅓ of the package of the yakisoba noodles in the skillet and sauté with about a tablespoon of *tonkatsu* sauce. Once heated through, transfer the noodles to a plate, wipe out the skillet, and pour a ladleful of batter onto the skillet and flatten into a pancake 6 to 8 inches/15 to 20.5 cm in diameter.

Place a pot lid over the batter to help it cook through. This will take about 4 minutes.

Remove the lid, and lay slices of thinly sliced pork on top of the pancake.

Flip the *okonomiyaki* and cook the pork until browned, 2 to 3 minutes.

With a spatula, flip the okonomiyaki onto the plate on top of the yakisoba, so that the browned pork is face up.

Let your guests top the *okonomiyaki* with *tonkatsu* sauce, mayonnaise, *aonori*, and other condiments. Enjoy!

LEXI'S FAVORITE MUSHROOM AND BEEF SAUCE

This is the most popular dinner request at our house. My family is *addicted* to this! Beef, mushrooms, and onions simmer in a buttery sauce spiked with a little bit of tangy mustard, making this dish hearty and comforting. It's similar to beef Stroganoff, but doesn't contain sour cream . . . and you'll never miss it! You can serve this over rice, pasta, or even some sautéed greens. I make a huge batch of this and just keep it in the freezer so our family can heat some up whenever we are in a crunch to make dinner. Trust me, you're going to want some of this on hand at all times!

YIELDS: **4 to 5 servings**
TIME: **30 minutes**

INGREDIENTS:

1 pound/455 g lean ground beef

½ teaspoon salt

½ teaspoon freshly ground black pepper

½ cup/1 stick/113 g unsalted butter (or a dairy-free butter alternative)

2 green onions, sliced (white and green parts)

2 tablespoons all-purpose flour

¼ cup/60 ml white wine

¾ cup/175 ml beef stock

12 ounces/340 g fresh cremini or white mushrooms, sliced

½ teaspoon prepared mustard

Salt and freshly ground black pepper

Pasta or rice for serving

Fresh parsley for garnish

DIRECTIONS:

In a large skillet over medium heat, brown the beef with ½ teaspoon each of salt and pepper until cooked through and crumbly. Transfer the beef to a plate and set aside.

In the same skillet, melt the butter and cook the green onions slowly for 3 to 5 minutes, scraping the browned bits off the bottom of the pan with a wooden spoon.

Stir in the flour and cook for a few minutes. Slowly whisk in the wine and deglaze the skillet. Add the stock and mushrooms, and bring to a boil, stirring occasionally. Lower the heat and simmer for about 15 minutes, until the mushrooms are cooked through.

Stir in the mustard and season with salt and pepper to taste.

Server over pasta or rice. Garnish with parsley.

LIME FISH TACOS WITH PICO DE GALLO AND CRUNCHY CABBAGE SLAW

These tacos are absolutely perfect for summer. They are light, fresh, and full of flavor, and you can enjoy the sun by grilling the fish outside on the barbecue. The first time I made these, my family devoured them, and they have been a staple in my house ever since. These tacos are filled with tender, flaky grilled fish, crunchy slaw, and a creamy and tangy pico de gallo. I could eat that pico de gallo with a spoon by itself, it's *so* good. . . .

YIELDS: **4 very small servings**
TIME: **1 hour**

INGREDIENTS:

Fish:

1½ pounds/680 g white flaky fish, such as cod

Salt and freshly ground black pepper

¼ cup/60 ml grapeseed oil

Juice of 1 lime

¼ cup/10 g fresh cilantro leaves, chopped

Pico de gallo:

1 avocado, peeled, pitted, and chopped into chunks

2 cups/360 g chopped tomato

¼ cup/40 g small-diced red onion

¼ cup/10 g fresh cilantro, chopped

3 tablespoons freshly squeezed lime juice (from 1 juicy lime)

¼ teaspoon fresh minced jalapeño pepper (optional)

Salt and freshly ground black pepper

Cabbage Slaw:

½ small head red cabbage, shredded thinly (about 4 heaping cups/300 g)

2 tablespoons mayonnaise

Juice of 1 lime

Fresh cilantro, chopped

Salt and freshly ground black pepper

Other:

Corn tortillas

Limes to squeeze on tacos

Fresh cilantro, chopped

DIRECTIONS:

Sprinkle both sides of the fish with salt and black pepper, and place it in a medium baking dish. Whisk together the oil, lime juice, and cilantro, and pour over the fish. Let marinate for 15 to 20 minutes.

In a bowl, mix together all the pico de gallo ingredients, seasoning with salt and black pepper to taste. Set aside.

In another bowl, mix together all the slaw ingredients, including chopped cilantro and salt and black pepper to taste. Set aside.

Preheat the grill to medium-high heat. Oil the grill to prevent the fish from sticking. Remove the fish from the marinade and place onto the hot grill. Grill the fish for 4 minutes on the first side and then flip and cook for 1 minute or so, depending on the thickness of the fish. Remove and let rest for 5 minutes. Flake the fish into bite-size pieces with a fork.

Place the corn tortillas on the grill and grill until heated through and they have nice grill marks.

Place the fish, pico de gallo, slaw, tortillas, and other garnishes on the table and let your guests fill their tortillas to their liking.

SALMON SALAD, AVOCADO, AND CUCUMBER SUSHI HAND ROLLS

Sushi is an art—people spend their entire lives mastering it! But the good news is, the rest of us can have mouthwatering sushi without any training. Sushi hand rolls are easy, fun, and healthy. The version I usually make isn't so traditional, though. I use brown rice instead of white and salmon salad is the main filling instead of raw fish. You can choose whatever sushi fillings you want, but this is my family's favorite version.

YIELDS: **4 servings (4 rolls per person)**
TIME: **20 minutes active + 3 hours 30 minutes for rice**

INGREDIENTS:

Sushi rice:

1 cup/190 g short-grain brown rice

1½ teaspoons salt

1 tablespoon sugar

1 tablespoon rice vinegar

Salmon salad:

2 (6-ounce/170 g) cans wild Alaskan salmon, drained

¼ cup/60 g mayonnaise

2 teaspoons freshly squeezed lemon juice

Salt and freshly ground black pepper

Toppings:

½ cucumber, cut into thin matchsticks

1 avocado, peeled, pitted, and sliced

Fresh chives or green onions, chopped

To assemble:

4 or more nori (seaweed) sheets

Condiments:

Wasabi (horseradish) paste

Pickled ginger

Soy sauce or tamari

DIRECTIONS:

Prepare the sushi rice: Place the rice in a large bowl and fill with plenty of water. Wash the rice in the water, then drain. Repeat 2 or 3 times.

Put the rice into a heavy pot with 1½ cups/355 ml of fresh water and let it sit for 2 to 3 hours.

With the pot lid slightly ajar, bring the water to a boil. Then, cover the pot, Lower the heat to its lowest setting, and let the rice simmer and absorb the water for 15 to 20 minutes.

Turn off the heat and let the rice steam, with the lid on, for another 10 minutes.

While the rice is cooking, place the salt, sugar, and vinegar in a small saucepan and cook over medium-low heat, until the sugar and salt have dissolved. Remove from the heat and let cool.

When the rice is done, fluff it up with a wooden spatula and scoop it onto a big plate or serving platter so there is a lot of surface area to help it cool faster.

While the rice is still hot, drizzle the vinegar mixture over it and gently mix the rice with a wooden spatula to cover each grain with the flavoring. Let it cool completely.

To keep the rice moist, cover with a damp towel.

Prepare the salmon salad: In a bowl, stir together the wild salmon, mayonnaise, lemon juice, and salt and pepper to taste. Feel free to add extra lemon juice if you want a little more tang.

Mix thoroughly until everything is combined.

To serve: Place all the ingredients on separate plates or in bowls.

Cut each nori sheet into four squares.

Everyone can assemble their own sushi rolls: Place some rice on a nori square, then the salmon salad topped with cucumber and avocado. Then, wrap the nori around the filling. It doesn't have to be perfect!

Serve with pickled ginger. Dip in soy sauce (with wasabi, if desired), and *eat*!

POACHED SALMON SALAD WITH GOAT CHEESE AND TARRAGON HERB DRESSING (A.K.A. I'M-IN-HEAVEN SALAD)

When I was four years old, I named this the I'm-in-Heaven Salad because it is so delicious—even at a young age, I could tell when I tasted a masterpiece! The cool thing about this salad is that it looks really fancy, but it's actually super simple to make. This salad is filled with amazing flavors from the fragrant dressing, tangy goat cheese, the bite from the onion, and the tender, poached salmon. I wasn't kidding when I named this dish.

YIELDS: **6 servings**
TIME: **30 minutes + chilling time**

INGREDIENTS:

Poached salmon:

4 (6-ounce/170 g salmon fillets, about 1-inch/2.5 cm thick

2 teaspoons salt

1 teaspoon freshly ground black pepper

About 2 cups/475 ml dry white wine

Dressing:

¼ cup/60 ml Champagne vinegar

1½ teaspoons Dijon mustard

½ teaspoon salt

¼ teaspoon freshly ground black pepper

½ cup/120 ml grapeseed oil

2 tablespoons minced fresh chives

2 tablespoons minced fresh tarragon

To assemble:

2 (5-ounce/140 g) packages mixed baby greens

½ red onion, sliced thinly with a mandoline

3 to 4 ounces/85 to 115 g goat cheese, crumbled (optional)

Chives for garnish (optional)

Zucchini for serving (optional; see directions)

DIRECTIONS:

Prepare the salmon: Place the salmon in a 10-inch/25.5 cm skillet. The salmon should fit tightly in the pan. This way it doesn't require as much wine to cover the fillets. Season the salmon with salt and pepper. Add enough wine to the skillet to cover the fillets. If the wine doesn't completely cover the fish, add water to make up the difference.

Cover and simmer over medium-low heat until the salmon is cooked, about 7 minutes. Using a spatula, transfer the salmon to a plate and refrigerate until chilled.

Prepare the dressing: In a bowl, stir together the vinegar, mustard, salt, and pepper. Add grapeseed oil in a steady stream while whisking until the dressing is well blended. Stir in the herbs.

Assemble the salad: In a bowl, combine the mixed greens and red onion. Break the salmon into big bite-size chunks, add the dressing, and toss to coat. Top with goat cheese and chives, if using, and serve immediately.

I love serving this salad in zucchini rings. To do this, use a mandoline to thinly slice a zucchini lengthwise into ribbons. Take two long ribbons and overlap the ends, creating a ring. If the ribbons don't stick, dabbing a little water on the ends will help. Place the circle on a plate, fill it with salad, top with goat cheese, and sprinkle with chives.

salmon

Salmon is one of my all-time favorite seafood items because it's so flavorful, really easy to cook, and it's good for you. It's an awesome source of healthy omega-3 fats and protein, which help build and repair muscles. So, to all you athletes out there: go get yourself some salmon!

SUKIYAKI (JAPANESE BEEF AND VEGETABLE STEW)

Sukiyaki is a delicious Japanese beef stew that you cook at the table as you eat. Thinly sliced beef, veggies, tofu, *mochi*, and mushrooms are cooked in a shallow pan by adding the ingredients one by one to the hot, bubbling broth. All the flavors come together beautifully, and it's absolutely delicious! After I had it for the first time in Japan, I asked my nana to teach me how to make it. I was really surprised at how easy it is! Thank you, Nana!

YIELDS: **4 to 6 servings**
TIME: **30 minutes to prep everything + cooking time as you go**

INGREDIENTS:

Broth:

1 cup/235 ml soy sauce

1 cup/235 ml mirin

½ cup/120 ml sake (should be good enough to drink—for an adult, of course!)

1 to 2 tablespoons sugar

Hot pot:

3 to 4 baby bok choy

12 ounces/340 g enoki mushrooms

2 to 3 fresh shiitake mushrooms

1 large onion

1 (12 ounce/340 g) package store-bought grilled tofu, cubed

1 (7-ounce/198 g) package fresh *shirataki* (yam noodles)

1 (7-ounce/198 g) package fresh udon noodles

1 pound/455 g beef, sliced into very thin strips (you can get this presliced at Asian supermarkets, or your butcher may slice them thinly for you)

4 pieces *mochi* (pounded rice cake)

To cook:

1 tablespoon grapeseed oil

DIRECTIONS:

Prepare the broth: Put all the broth ingredients plus ½ cup/120 ml of water into a saucepan and bring to a boil. Keep stirring until the sugar is dissolved. Lower the heat to low and keep at a simmer while you prepare the rest of your ingredients.

Prepare the hot pot ingredients: Cut off the bottom of each baby bok choy; wash and separate the leaves.

Clean the mushrooms. Trim the base of the enoki mushrooms and cut the stems off the shiitake mushrooms.

Peel and cut the onion in half, then slice thinly into half-moons.

Wash the tofu and slice into bite-size pieces.

Submerge the *shirataki* in a saucepan of cold water. Bring to a boil, let boil for 4 minutes, and drain. The noodles are very long, so cut them shorter, using clean kitchen scissors.

If the udon noodles are stiff and stuck together after taking them out of the packaging, submerge them in lukewarm water to break apart.

Put all the prepped hot pot ingredients, plus the beef and mochi, in separate heaps on a large serving platter so everything is ready to cook.

To cook: At the table, coat the bottom of your hot pot or electric skillet with oil and heat. Once it is hot, add some of the onion and sauté until translucent. Add some of the beef and let it brown. Pour in enough broth to almost cover the beef and onion.

Move the beef and onion aside and add the *shirataki*, tofu, and mushrooms. Cover and cook until the veggies are tender. As the veggies and beef cook, they add to the flavor of the broth, which soaks into the food. Delicious!

The udon and *mochi* tend to soak up a lot of liquid, so wait until the end of cooking to add those. Cook the *mochi* until it is super soft and gooey. You will need a spoon to scoop it out.

As you cook, much of the liquid will evaporate, intensifying the flavor of the broth. Add water as you go to prevent it from becoming too strong. Feel free to add more mirin or sake to balance out the flavor as you like.

Sukiyaki is eaten as its ingredients cook. To serve, scoop out of the pot and into your bowl whatever ingredients you want and drizzle the broth on top. Continue adding ingredients to the pot to cook until all of it is cooked and enjoyed by everyone.

ONE-POT PASTA WITH TOMATOES, GREENS, AND GARLIC

An amazing dinner *and* fewer dishes to clean? What else could you want?! This pasta is amazing because all you do is throw all the ingredients in one pot, including the dried pasta, and let the flavors come together as it cooks. The greens soak up the garlic and tomato, and are actually my favorite part of this pasta. Oh, and did I mention that you only have to wash one pot? (My dad, who is in charge of washing dishes, is always extremely happy about that part.)

YIELDS: **6 to 8 servings**
TIME: **30 minutes**

INGREDIENTS:

1½ to 2 pounds/680 to 905 g ripe tomatoes

8 ounces/225 g kale

8 ounces/225 g chard

½ cup/120 ml plus 1 tablespoon olive oil, divided, plus more for serving

2 garlic cloves, peeled and pressed

5 cups/1.2 L low-sodium chicken or vegetable stock (or 4 cups/946 ml stock plus 1 cup/235 ml water)

Pinch of red pepper flakes

2 teaspoons salt, plus more for serving

1 pound/455 g dried spaghetti

¼ cup/10 g fresh basil, sliced into thin ribbons

Freshly ground black pepper

DIRECTIONS:

Roughly chop the tomatoes. Stem the kale and chard and rip them into bite-size pieces.

Grab a pot that is big enough for the spaghetti to lay flat at the bottom (you can also break the pasta in half if you don't have a big enough pot).

Add a tablespoon of the olive oil and the garlic to the pot. Let the garlic sauté for a minute over medium heat and then add the stock. Bring to a boil.

Once the stock comes to a boil, add the red pepper flakes, remaining ½ cup/120 ml of oil, and salt.

Add the pasta, making sure it is all submerged in the water. Give it a stir. Add the tomatoes.

Let the pasta simmer for about 6 minutes, stirring occasionally so the noodles don't stick.

Add the kale and chard, and let cook a bit more until the spaghetti is al dente, about 2 minutes.

Season with salt and black pepper to taste. Serve with olive oil drizzled on top and sprinkle with fresh basil.

garlic

Garlic isn't just for warding off vampires. It can be spicy when raw, but when cooked, it turns sweet and savory, instantly taking a dish to the next level. Not only is a clove of garlic packed with flavor, but it's also full of calcium, which helps keep your bones strong and your muscles working properly. If you play sports as I do, garlic will be your secret weapon!

CAULIFLOWER, TOMATO, AND CHICKPEA CURRY

This is one of my mom's favorite dishes. She got so excited when I was filming a video for my YouTube channel featuring this recipe, because she knew she would get the leftovers! This curry is creamy, with sweetness from the tomatoes, and the chickpeas and cauliflower add an earthy savoriness to the dish. It's filling and hearty even without any meat, and it's such a great way to get a ton of veggies! Everyone in my family always has seconds when I make this for dinner.

YIELDS: **6 servings**

TIME: **1 hour (if you prep the onions and chickpeas while the veggies are roasting)**

INGREDIENTS:

3 tablespoons plus 1 teaspoon grapeseed oil, divided

½ head cauliflower, cut into bite-size pieces (about 3 heaping cups)

2½ cups/375 g cherry tomatoes (or regular tomatoes, sliced)

Salt and freshly ground black pepper

1 large yellow onion, chopped

3 garlic cloves, peeled and pressed

1 tablespoon grated fresh ginger

4 teaspoons yellow curry powder

2 (15-ounce/425 ml) cans chickpeas (about 3 cups/300 g), drained and rinsed

2 cups/475 ml chicken or vegetable stock

2 tablespoons unsalted butter (or a dairy-free butter alternative)

3 to 5 cups/90 to 150 g baby spinach

Cooked basmati rice for serving

Fresh parsley for garnish

DIRECTIONS:

Preheat the oven to 375°F/190°C.

Toss the cauliflower in 2 teaspoons of the oil and place on a baking sheet. Do the same with the tomatoes on another baking sheet. Make sure they are in a single layer and not crowded. Season both with salt and pepper, and roast for about 25 minutes the oven. This intensifies the flavor and gets rid of some moisture.

In a medium pot, heat the remaining 2 tablespoons of oil over medium-high heat. Cook the onion until golden brown, about 10 minutes. Then, add the garlic, ginger, and curry powder. Cook until fragrant, about 1 minute.

Add the tomatoes, chickpeas, and stock and bring to a boil. Simmer, uncovered, over medium-low heat until the liquid is thickened and flavors are blended, about 30 minutes. Be patient, because it doesn't taste like much while it's still watery!

Add the cauliflower and simmer until it is warmed through and soft but not mushy.

Add the butter, which gives the curry a rich, creamy flavor, and salt and pepper to taste. If your tomatoes are really sweet, you will need more salt—this is really important!

Stir in the spinach and let it wilt. Season with salt and pepper to taste.

Serve over rice and sprinkle with parsley.

cauliflower

Did you know cauliflower is known as a superfood? It's a good source of healthy omega-3 fatty acids, fiber, and tons of vitamin C. Good thing it's available year-round and that it's versatile and delicious. I have several recipes in this book that use cauliflower . . . so clearly, I'm a fan.

satisfy your sweet tooth

Sweets that Are Parent Approved

You may think that all dessert recipes have to be packed with sugar, making them bad for you. But I'm breaking that stereotype with some awesome dessert recipes that will satisfy your sweet tooth *and* leave you feeling good.

COLD BERRIES WITH
WARM VANILLA SAUCE

Hot, sweet, white chocolate and vanilla sauce drizzled over cold, tart, half-frozen berries . . . this is the ultimate dessert that's fancy enough to serve for company. It's so easy to make and yet it is super sophisticated. You even get the benefits of healthy berries, which is a bonus! When I was younger, this was my mom's go-to dessert for when we had company—and I'm not gonna lie; I totally tried to lick the plate when nobody was looking.

YIELDS: **4 servings**
TIME: **10 minutes**

INGREDIENTS:

5 ounces/140 g white chocolate chips

1½ teaspoons pure vanilla extract

½ cup/120 ml heavy whipping cream

1 pound/455 g frozen mixed berries, such as blueberries, blackberries, strawberries, or marionberries

DIRECTIONS:

Prepare a double boiler by simmering a few inches/cm of water in a saucepan and placing a heat-safe bowl over the pan. Make sure the bowl is not touching the simmering water.

Put the white chocolate chips, vanilla, and cream in the bowl and keep stirring until everything is melted and super silky and smooth.

Place the frozen berries on a plate and drizzle the hot white chocolate over top.

DARK CHOCOLATE COCONUT FONDUE

Who doesn't love dipping stuff in chocolate? I know I do! I made this special treat on the *E! Live from the Red Carpet* preshow for the Oscars a few years ago, and everybody was in awe! This creamy, chocolaty fondue uses coconut milk instead of heavy cream, and high-quality dark chocolate. The gorgeous coconut cream swirl adds a delicate touch. This is definitely an Oscar-worthy dish.

YIELDS: **A little over 2 cups/475 ml, serves 8**
TIME: **10 minutes**

INGREDIENTS:

Favorite dipping fruits, such as bananas, strawberries, blueberries, raspberries, or grapes

1 (14-ounce/400 g) can coconut milk (not coconut beverage), divided

2 teaspoons pure vanilla extract

2 cups/350 g high-quality dark chocolate chips

DIRECTIONS:

Prepare a double boiler by simmering a few inches of water/cm in a saucepan and placing a heat-safe bowl over the pan. Make sure the bowl is not touching the simmering water.

While the water is coming to a simmer, wash and cut your fruits so they are bite-size. Arrange them on a plate.

Scoop out about a tablespoon of the coconut cream (the thick stuff at the top of the can when you open it) and set aside.

Pour about ⅔ of what remains in the can into the bowl, along with the vanilla and chocolate chips. Stir and let the chocolate melt until smooth and creamy. Add more coconut milk if you prefer a thinner fondue. Pour the chocolate into a fondue pot.

Melt the reserved coconut cream. You can do this in another (smaller) double boiler or replace the chocolate bowl with a new bowl. It will not take very long for the cream to melt and become smooth.

Drizzle the coconut cream on top of the chocolate in a swirl. Taking a toothpick, swirl the coconut cream in the chocolate, creating a pretty design.

Serve with fondue picks or bamboo skewers. Dip the fruit into the chocolate, and enjoy!

RASPBERRY ICE CREAM IN A DARK CHOCOLATE BOWL

This dessert is simple but absolutely stunning and elegant. The combo of the sweet, tart, creamy, vibrant raspberry ice cream with the crunchy, rich, dark chocolate bowl is going to wow all your friends and family. Plus, how cool is it to say that you made the dessert *and* the bowl?!

YIELDS: 8 servings
TIME: 45 active + several hours cooling time for the bowls

YOU WILL NEED:

8 water balloons

INGREDIENTS:

10 ounces/280 g dark chocolate

2 cups/500 g frozen raspberries

1 cup/235 ml almond milk

4 frozen bananas

Fresh mint sprigs for garnish (optional)

DIRECTIONS:

Wash 8 water balloons and blow up each to about the size of a baseball.

Prepare a double boiler by simmering a few inches/cm of water in a saucepan and placing a heat-safe bowl over the pan. Make sure the bowl is not touching the simmering water.

Melt the chocolate in the bowl until it's silky smooth. Place small little dollops of chocolate on a silicone mat. Dip the bottom half of each balloon into the bowl of chocolate and place it on the dollop of chocolate on the mat. Place all the balloons on the dollops and let sit until they are completely hardened, about 3 hours.

Once hardened, snip the tops of the balloons to pop them and carefully pull each balloon away from the wall of your chocolate bowl. If there is a small hole at the bottom of your chocolate bowl, add some more chocolate and let sit for another 20 minutes.

To make the ice cream, blend together the raspberries, almond milk, and bananas in a blender until smooth. Scoop the ice cream into the chocolate bowls and garnish with fresh mint sprigs. If you freeze the ice cream, it will get really hard, so let it sit out for about 30 minutes before scooping and serving.

MANGO RASPBERRY COCONUT SORBET

I love light, refreshing, fruity desserts, especially my sorbet. This is something you'll want to make over and over again. My recipe really shows off the sweet mango, which is complimented by tart raspberries and silky coconut milk. It's a great treat on a hot day, and you can even serve it as an elegant dessert at a party!

YIELDS: **5 servings**
TIME: **15 minutes + freezing time**

INGREDIENTS:

5 cups/825 g frozen mango

1 (14-ounce/400 g can coconut milk (not coconut beverage)

½ teaspoon freshly grated lemon zest

1 teaspoon freshly squeezed lemon juice

Pinch of salt

¾ cup/150 g sugar

½ teaspoon pure vanilla extract

½ cup/120 ml almond milk

1 cup/250 g frozen raspberries, divided

coconut

Coconut is really an overachiever because people all over the world use its flesh, water, and oil for cooking, baking, beauty routines, and even medicinal purposes. Coconuts are a source of fiber, vitamins, minerals, and calcium, and we humans try our best to take advantage of all of these—you'll see coconut oil and coconut milk used in many of the recipes in this book, too. People even use it as a makeup remover and skin moisturizer. Sounds like a superfood to me!

DIRECTIONS:

Put the frozen mango in a food processor along with coconut milk (the cream as well as the water), lemon zest and juice, salt, sugar, vanilla, and almond milk. Start by pulsing the mixture in the food processor, then process until smooth.

Pulse in ½ of the raspberries. Make sure there are still chunks.

Pour the mixture into a baking dish and freeze for 5 or more hours.

Scoop out into bowls, garnish with leftover frozen raspberries, and enjoy!

TIP

wait, i can have dessert?!

Yes, you can! Sometimes desserts are packed with sugar, but the great thing about making your own desserts is that you can choose healthy substitutions for all that sugar. This way, you can satisfy your sweet tooth without putting your health on the back burner. Here are my favorite substitutes:

HONEY OR DATES RATHER THAN WHITE SUGAR: Honey and dates are whole foods and aren't processed.

DARK CHOCOLATE INSTEAD OF MILK CHOCOLATE: Dark chocolate contains more cacao, which is a superfood, and it has less cream and sugar than milk chocolate.

FRUIT INSTEAD OF HIGH-SUGAR DESSERT TOPPINGS: Sometimes fresh berries and chopped peaches are tastier toppings on ice cream, pancakes, or cupcakes than chemical-filled sprinkles and chocolate sauces. The fruit is sweet but also adds a great freshness to the dessert.

drinks

Special Sips

Ditch the sugary sodas and get ready to sip on these babies. The following drink recipes are so incredibly simple to make, they look gorgeous, and they use all-natural sweeteners. Make them for parties or just when you want to enjoy something special at home.

CLEMENTINE AND MANGO YOGURT SMOOTHIE

This is a clementine-inspired recipe from when I visited the grove in California. Up until then, I never thought to put clementines in my smoothies, but holy moly, now I'm hooked! Clementines are very similar to oranges, but they are a bit sweeter and have an awesome tartness to them. They add such a refreshing, tanginess to this drink. Sweet, tart, and creamy, this smoothie is great any time of day, whether it's for breakfast, snack, or dessert.

YIELDS: **2 servings**
TIME: **5 minutes**

INGREDIENTS:

4 clementines, peeled

½ cup/83 g frozen mango

¼ cup/60 g vanilla or plain yogurt

1 tablespoon honey, or to taste

4 to 5 large ice cubes (optional)

DIRECTIONS:

Blend together all the ingredients in a blender until smooth. You can add ice for a super cold, thicker smoothie.

Serve in a glass with a straw, or if you made it really thick, you can enjoy it with a spoon.

LAVENDER LEMONADE

You may have tried peach lemonade, strawberry lemonade, or raspberry lemonade . . . but have you ever tried *lavender* lemonade?! It is my favorite flavor. Both kids and adults will love this twist on a traditional summer drink. It's fragrant, tangy, sweet, and heavenly.

YIELDS: **6 cups**
TIME: **30 minutes + chilling time**

INGREDIENTS:

¼ cup/6 g dried culinary-grade lavender buds

1 cup/235 ml freshly squeezed lemon juice (from 4 to 6 lemons)

3 cups/710 ml cold water

¾ to 1 teaspoon pure liquid stevia extract

Ice for serving

DIRECTIONS:

Bring 2 cups/475 ml of water to a simmer in a small pot. Add the lavender, remove from the heat, and steep for 20 minutes. Strain.

In a pitcher, combine the lavender water, lemon juice, and the cold water.

Stir in ¾ teaspoon of stevia extract. If you want a sweeter lemonade, add the remaining ¼ teaspoon of stevia. Pour into a glass with ice and enjoy!

To make with sugar: Add ¾ to 1 cup/150 to 200 g of sugar (depending on taste) to the simmering water and stir to dissolve. Proceed with the recipe, omitting stevia.

WATERMELON MINT SLUSHY

Slushies are a great way to cool off in the summer, but whenever you get a slushy from the store, it usually looks like it can glow in the dark! My version uses all-natural ingredients and still has that fruity, sweet, refreshing taste that I crave. There are many flavors of slushies out there, but you gotta try my watermelon version. The mint adds freshness and pairs really well with the sweet, juicy watermelon.

YIELDS: **2 servings**
TIME: **5 minutes**

INGREDIENTS:

4 cups/600 g cubed watermelon

2 sprigs of fresh mint

Juice of ½ lime

1 tablespoon honey

About 6 large ice cubes

DIRECTIONS:

Place the watermelon, mint, lime, and honey in a blender and blend until smooth.

Add 2 ice cubes at a time and blend. Keep adding ice cubes until the slushy becomes thick and frothy.

Serve in a glass with a straw and top it off with a sprig of mint.

ICED ORANGE AND GREEN TEA

I love this iced tea because it's refreshing, fragrant, and light. It will definitely quench your thirst and cool you down on a hot summer's day.

YIELDS: **1 big or 2 small servings**
TIME: **10 minutes + chilling time**

INGREDIENTS:

1 cup/235 ml boiling water

1 green tea bag

1 tablespoon freshly squeezed lemon juice

2 cups/475 ml freshly squeezed orange juice

DIRECTIONS:

Pour the boiling water into a heatproof bowl and add the green tea bag. Let the tea steep for a few minutes.

Pour the tea into a pitcher along with the lemon juice and orange juice. Add a big handful of ice cubes (4 to 5 cubes) and chill in the fridge before serving.

green tea

I love waking up in the morning and having a cup of tea. My all-time favorite is green tea, because it increases your focus and energy, and it is also said to speed up your metabolism, which helps burn fat. I like to drink it with a few drops of liquid stevia. It's perfect for an early school morning, before a workout, or while studying for a big exam.

recipes for hair and skin

Feeding Your Body from the Outside

We all want glowing skin and silky smooth hair, but store-bought products can get pricy *and* can contain lots of artificial ingredients. Don't worry, because I have five all-natural homemade beauty remedies that won't break the bank and you will know exactly what goes into each. I want to make sure that we all take care of our bodies on the inside *and* the outside.

SILKY HAIR MASK

Hair masks are great for bringing some life back into your hair. They make hair soft, healthy, and smooth, which is what everybody wants! Here is how you make your very own hair mask at home. This recipe is great because olive oil and oats are super moisturizing; honey has antioxidant properties, which helps prevent hair damage; and avocado is a perfect way to nourish your hair and scalp to keep everything soft and healthy.

YIELDS: 1 treatment
TIME: 5 minutes

INGREDIENTS:

¼ cup/20 g rolled oats

1 avocado, peeled and pitted

2 tablespoons olive oil

1 tablespoon honey

DIRECTIONS:

In a food processor or electric spice/coffee grinder, pulse the oatmeal until it is a powder.

Mash the avocado in a bowl with a fork until there are no clumps.

Add the olive oil, honey, and oat powder and mix until combined.

Apply to your hair and let the mask sit in your hair for 30 minutes to an hour and then rinse out with warm water.

Shampoo and condition your hair as usual. Apply to hair once a week.

ACNE-TAMING CINNAMON FACE MASK

Store-bought face masks can get really expensive! Here is an effective mask that you can make at home. This mask is made with cinnamon, which is an antibacterial and can fight against acne-causing bacteria. The lemon juice helps tone your face skin for an even complexion, and the honey kills bacteria and clears your pores. The cinnamon tingles when you put it on, but that's how you know it's working! Since some people can have a bad reaction to cinnamon, it's a good idea to patch test it first behind your ear. I use this mask about once a week and it has really helped my skin.

YIELDS: 2 tablespoons, about 2 face masks
TIME: 5 minutes

INGREDIENTS:

1½ teaspoons ground cinnamon

1 teaspoon freshly grated nutmeg

1 tablespoon honey

½ teaspoon freshly squeezed lemon juice

DIRECTIONS:

Mix all the ingredients together in a small bowl.

Apply a thin layer over your face and let sit for 15 to 20 minutes. (It may drip, so try not to make any crazy movements.)

Rinse off with warm water. Store the rest of the mask in an airtight container in the fridge for up to 2 weeks. If the mask has thickened for subsequent uses, add a bit more honey or lemon juice to get to your desired consistency.

CLEANSING BODY SCRUB

Exfoliating your body is just as important as exfoliating your face. It leaves your skin smooth, glowing, and super soft. The lemon in this scrub keeps bacteria at bay and helps tone the skin, and the honey moisturizes your entire body. Bonus: this cleansing body scrub smells like coconut lemon bars! *Yes, please!* I use this scrub a few times a week, and I come out of the shower feeling so moisturized I don't even have to put on lotion.

YIELDS: **1½ cups/about 500 g, enough for 5 to 10 treatments**
TIME: **5 minutes**

INGREDIENTS:

¼ cup/60 ml freshly squeezed lemon juice

Zest of 2 lemons

1 cup/225 g brown sugar

1 cup/200 g granulated sugar

1 tablespoon honey

2 tablespoons melted coconut oil

DIRECTIONS:

Mix all the ingredients together.

Pour into a pint-size mason jar and let sit in the fridge for 20 minutes or so until the coconut oil solidifies.

Take a big handful of scrub and gently massage it all over your body or the parts you want to exfoliate. Rinse off with water. Store leftover scrub in the fridge for up to 2 weeks.

GENTLE FACE SCRUB

Exfoliating your face is important because it removes all the dead skin cells so you are left with healthy, glowing skin. But why buy exfoliating scrubs when you can make your own at home with ingredients that most of you already have sitting in your pantry?

Here's my favorite face scrub that is gentle but still effective. The scrub has lemon for toning and sugar to remove dead skin cells so that your skin feels rejuvenated and like new. I use this scrub every night before bed, and I go to sleep with super-soft skin.

YIELDS: **2 cups/about 300 g, about 10 scrubs**
TIME: **5 minutes**

INGREDIENTS:

1 cup/200 g granulated sugar

2 tablespoons honey

1½ teaspoons ground cinnamon

¼ cup/60 ml freshly squeezed lemon juice

1 tablespoon coconut oil

DIRECTIONS:

Mix all the ingredients together in a bowl.

Wet your face and massage a small palmful of the scrub all over your face.

Rinse off with warm water. Store the leftover face mask in a mason jar and keep in the fridge for up to 2 weeks.

NO-FRIZZ OIL TREATMENT

If you're like me, and you can't stand frizzy hair, then this oil treatment is going to be your new best friend. It makes your hair silky, shiny, and frizz-free, and it only requires two ingredients! The coconut oil and olive oil moisturize your hair and keep it healthy and super soft. It's amazing!

YIELDS: **1 treatment, depending on the length of your hair**
TIME: **5 minutes**

INGREDIENTS:

3 tablespoons coconut oil

3 tablespoons olive oil

DIRECTIONS:

Place the coconut oil in a microwave-safe bowl and microwave it for 15 seconds at a time on HIGH, mixing in between until fully melted.

Add the olive oil and mix together until the oils are combined.

Working in sections, take chunks of your hair and massage the oil mixture into the strands. Make sure to massage from the roots all the way to the ends.

Keep adding the oil until your whole head is shiny (you should look like you haven't showered in a month). Tie your hair up and let the oil soak into your hair for 2 to 3 hours.

Shampoo the oil out of your hair. This may take two shampooings. Apply conditioner as usual, and rinse.

TIP

my skincare routine

I have been struggling with acne since I was in fifth grade. I was (and still am) super self-conscious about my skin. I felt like the acne was all people would ever see on my face. Thankfully, I have gotten a better idea of how to tame my skin over the years. I want to share my tips and skincare routine with everyone, because I know that so many teens struggle with acne! Trust me when I say, you are not alone. Everybody's skin is different so what works for me may not work for you, but hopefully you will find at least one tip that will help you fight the acne battle.

KEEP YOUR FACE CLEAN. This one is pretty self-explanatory. I wash my face twice a day for my skin to stay clean, but you can wash it as many times as you feel works for you.

DON'T TOUCH YOUR FACE. I have a really bad habit of resting my fingers on my temples when I'm bored in class (it happens a lot). Because of this habit, I used to break out really badly on the sides of my face. So, try to keep your hands away as much as possible!

EAT CLEAN FOODS. Not only will eating fresh, wholesome, organic foods make you feel better, but it will clear up your skin, too! The better the ingredients you put in your body, the better your body will look and feel.

TRY AVOIDING DAIRY. The biggest thing that has cleared up my skin is not eating dairy. Now, I am not saying that I am totally dairy-free because I do love my cheese . . . but whenever my skin gets especially bad, it is usually because I have been eating too many dairy products. If you suspect dairy might be making you break out, try going without it for a while and see how it affects your skin.

MOISTURIZE. No joke, every night I go to bed looking like a little grease ball. Some people may think, "Oh, I have oily skin so I don't need to moisturize," but actually, if you don't moisturize, your skin starts to think that it's drying out so it has to produce more natural oil, thus making your skin oily. So, moisturizing your skin may help it go back to making its normal amount of oil.

STAY ON A ROUTINE. If you're constantly switching skin products and sometimes moisturizing and other days you're not, your skin is going to get confused and you won't be giving it enough time to heal. It takes up to 30 days for your skin to heal, rejuvenate, and create new skin, so give it some time.

Here is my typical hair and
skincare routine:

MORNING:
- Wash face with a gentle cleanser.
- Apply moisturizer.

NIGHT:
- Remove makeup, if wearing any. I use coconut oil to do this—just massage it in and wipe it off with a tissue.
- Use a gentle face scrubbing brush with an oil cleanser all over my face. Rinse.
- Apply an exfoliating scrub—my Gentle Face Scrub is perfect! Rinse.
- Apply toner and moisturizer.

EVERY WEEK:
- Apply Taming Face Mask.
- Apply No-Frizz Oil Treatment.

EVERY OTHER WEEK:
- Apply Silky Hair Mask.

Taking the time to care for my skin is really worth it for me. It helps my skin stay clear and my nighttime routine allows me to start winding down and relax. It's a peaceful way to end the night!

thank you!

MOM: If I didn't have you by my side, this book would not have happened. Period. You are truly the best writing partner I could possibly have. You kept me on schedule and on task, and edited every single line of this book. You're the glue to this whole operation and you always do it with grace and ease. You're like a modern-day superwoman! I am so grateful for everything you do for me. I know I can be a total pain in the butt and a moody teenage mess sometimes, but you stand by me through it all, and I can't express how much that means to me. You are my hero and my inspiration, and I love you so much!

DAD: Thank you, thank you, thank you. For all the late nights spent editing, for running to the grocery store when I needed to test a recipe, and for cleaning up the tornado I left behind in the kitchen! You have taught me some of the most valuable life lessons throughout this experience, and I am so grateful.

LEXI: You are the best sister a girl could ever ask for. People always say we are the closest sisters they have ever met, and I wouldn't want it any other way. You are my little sister, best friend, and partner for life. Writing this cookbook was the hardest project I have ever done, and whenever I got overwhelmed or stressed, I knew I could come to you to make me feel better. Thank you for always supporting me (whether it's with school, cooking, volleyball, or . . . boys), for belting out our favorite songs together, and for making me laugh harder than anyone on earth. I love you, Lexi Lou!

COOK WITH
AMBER

JAMIE OLIVER: I grew up with your cookbooks, watching your shows, and wanting to be like you. You were one of the reasons I started cooking in the first place. Fast forward a few years . . . being part of your Food Tube family, cooking alongside you, and chatting with you about wholesome cooking for kids . . . those are memories I will treasure for a lifetime. Thank you for teaching me everything from knife skills, to staying true to myself and my food style.

MY MENTORS: THE FOOD TUBE FAMILY, RACHAEL RAY, GUY FIERI, DONAL SKEHAN, TIA MOWRY, AND EVERYONE AT Q13 FOX NEWS: Thank you for teaching me the ways of this industry and for supporting my love of cooking. You all have given me such amazing guidance, and I am so grateful. I have had such great experiences and learned so much from each of you. Thank you. I wouldn't be here today without every single one of you.

MY BFFS: First off, I love you all more than you will ever know. You guys kept me sane through this crazy process. Thank you all for believing in me, almost more than I believe in myself, and for always finding a way to make me laugh.

KELLEY AND FUKUDA CLANS: To my amazing family . . . you all are my biggest support system and I know I can always come to you. You all have given me so much love, advice, and support over the years. Thank you for shaping me into the person I am today.

CLAIRE: You are the reason everything runs so smoothly around here! Not only do you help me stay organized and keep my "Cook with Amber" life on track, but you have such amazing ideas and tips on how to grow and improve. I would honestly be a mess without your guidance and organization skills. Thank you so much for joining the team and becoming a part of this family.

LUCY, RECIPE TESTER EXTRAORDINAIRE: Going through all of these recipes isn't easy, but you sure made it look that way. Thank you for finding all of our mistakes, teaching us the ways of recipe writing, and making these recipes better than ever before.

DAVID AND MARK OF ABRAMS ARTISTS: You guys are the ones who brought this all together. Thank you so much for getting me this insane opportunity and helping me spread my message. I am so grateful to have you guys on the team!

JULIE AND FRANCES OF RUNNING PRESS: Thank you for taking a chance on me and my message and for making my dreams come true. Because of you, I can now spread my love of cooking with the whole world through this book.

OLIVIA AND MCKENZIE: A cookbook is nothing without gorgeous food photos and you exceeded all expectations! Not only are you guys amazing at what you do, but you also made the experience so much fun and you taught me so much. Thank you!

THE AMAZING "COOK WITH AMBER" COMMUNITY: This is all for you! More than anything I hope this book gets you in the kitchen and having fun. Thank you guys for being so supportive of this project and keeping me inspired. I love you all!

index

Note: Page references in *italics* indicate recipe photographs.

188

e

196

197

Running Press Teens
Hachette Book Group
1290 Avenue of the Americas, New York, NY 10104
www.runningpress.com/rpkids
@RP_Kids

Printed in China

First Edition: October 2018

Published by Running Press Teens, an imprint of Perseus Books, LLC,
a subsidiary of Hachette Book Group, Inc. The Running Press Teens name
and logo is a trademark of the Hachette Book Group.

The Hachette Speakers Bureau provides a wide range of authors for speaking events.
To find out more, go to www.hachettespeakersbureau.com or call (866) 376-6591.

The publisher is not responsible for websites (or their content)
that are not owned by the publisher.

Print book cover and interior design by Frances J. Soo Ping Chow.
Food stylist: McKenzie Johnson
Additional photographs: p.12 © Getty Images/nata_vkusidey, p.34 © Getty Images/Jaynerr,
p.66 © Getty Images/villagemoon, p.108 © Getty Images/LFGabel,
p.164 © Getty Images/fcafotodigital

Library of Congress Control Number: 2017963213

ISBNs: 978-0-7624-6387-9 (paperback), 978-0-7624-6386-2 (ebook)

1010

10 9 8 7 6 5 4 3 2 1

To my sister Lexi—my best friend
and sidekick for life. You mean the world
to me, and I love you so much.

COOK WITH
AMBER

FUN, FRESH RECIPES to get you in the kitchen

amber kelley

Award-winning teen chef and star of the
online series "Cook with Amber"

RP|TEENS
PHILADELPHIA